MIKE SALTER

Discovering
Scottish Castles

A gazetteer of 1,026 castles

SHIRE PUBLICATIONS LTD

ACKNOWLEDGEMENTS

Photographs are acknowledged as follows: Cadbury Lamb, plates 2, 4-7, 9, 10, 24-26, front cover; Mike Salter, plates 3, 8, 11-14, 16-18, 20-23; Geoffrey N. Wright, plates 1, 15, 19. The plans (figures 1-3) are also by the author.

Cover photograph: *Caerlaverock Castle, Nithsdale District, Dumfries and Galloway.*

British Library Cataloguing in Publication data available.

Set in 9 point Times roman and printed in Great Britain by C. I. Thomas & Sons (Haverfordwest) Ltd, Press Buildings, Merlins Bridge, Haverfordwest.

Contents

Introduction

The word 'castle' originally meant a building with a dual function as both a private residence and a stronghold. In Scotland almost all the surviving lordly country residences built between 1100 and the 1630s had such a dual function, and all of them, with a few slightly later buildings with castellated features, are mentioned in the gazetteer.

During the reign of David I (1124-53), when the Western and Northern Isles were still under Norse domination, Normans from England were invited to take up estates in Scotland. A new society was established in which French became the court language, and Norman laws and customs began to replace Gaelic culture. Notable among the new customs were succession by primogeniture and feudalism, in which land was held in return for some kind of service, usually military, to an overlord, as defined in charters. Along with these new concepts went the castle, from which an estate was administered. Very few of the earliest castles were of stone, consisting instead of a mound (called a motte) wholly or partly made of material dug from a surrounding ditch, and having a palisaded enclosure around a timber house on the summit. Sometimes at the base was an enclosure (a bailey) with its own ditch, rampart, stockade and timber buildings for retainers, produce and animals. Impressive earthworks of such castles can be seen at The Mote of Urr in Galloway and Inverurie in Grampian.

Timber is vulnerable to both fire and water and by the thirteenth century it was fashionable to build stronger and more impressive castles in which stone or timber buildings in the bailey were surrounded by high stone curtain walls thick enough to have a wall-walk on top of them. Mingary and Tioram castles on the west coast are small and simple but others like Kildrummy in Grampian and Bothwell in Strathclyde were larger and had various round towers flanking the walls. In these latter castles one tower was bigger than the others and formed a donjon or keep acting as the citadel and residence of the lord. These keeps contained a dark cellar at ground level, a hall or living room above, and one or more private rooms above that. Some castles of this period had impressive gateways, often with a tower on either side of the passage, as at Caerlaverock in Dumfries and Galloway, where it also functioned as a keep. Most of these early stone castles suffered sieges and eventual destruction by the Scots themselves during their struggles, known as the Wars of Independence, against the domineering English kings Edward I, II and III, from 1296 to the 1340s.

Rectangular keeps could be built on their own without significant outer defences, and castles of this kind, called tower

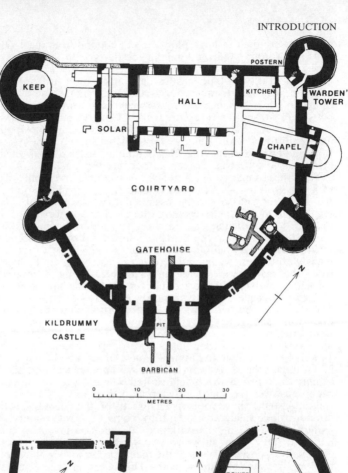

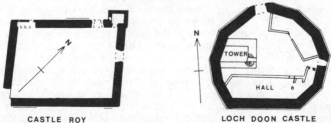

Fig. 1. Thirteenth-century castles of enclosure. Castle Roy (Badenoch and Strathspey District) and Loch Doon Castle (Cumnock and Doon Valley District) are small and simple, but Kildrummy Castle (Gordon District) is a more complex structure with a round tower keep, other towers, substantial domestic buildings, and a gatehouse with twin D-shaped towers.

houses, were built in huge numbers in Scotland from the 1360s onwards, forming the predominant castle type in the country. Scotland was comparatively poor and has only a few late medieval courtyard-type castles, a single tower with a few outbuildings being adequate for accommodating the households of most lairds. Examples of massive plain tower houses of between 1370 and 1450 are Threave and Comlongon in Dumfries and Galloway, Craigmillar and Borthwick in Lothian, Neidpath in the Borders and Drum in Grampian. Some of these are L-planned with a projecting wing containing extra rooms, which increase the otherwise rather limited accommodation.

There are so many towers in Scotland dating from about 1500 to about 1610 that castles not assigned to a particular period in the gazetteer entries can be assumed to be of this era. The secularisation of extensive church lands at the Reformation of the 1550s in particular caused a castle-building boom. It was during this period that the Scots developed a distinctive secular architectural style, building tower houses on a wide variety of plans with towers, wings and turrets projected out at all angles from the main block, with an extensive use of decorative corbelling and mouldings to support projecting upper parts. These castles have only one entrance secured by a yett, grilles or bars on accessible windows, loops for pistols and moderately thick walls strengthened by vaulting over the cellars, but they were intended only to withstand sudden raids by outlaws and malicious neighbours, not sieges by properly equipped armies. Towers like Amisfield in Dumfries and Galloway and Craigievar in Grampian have a 'fairy-tale' castle appearance with their summits adorned with conical-roofed round bartizans, square caphouses over the stairs and stepped gables rising to chimney stacks. Also they have roofs rising directly off the side walls, with dormer windows lighting the top rooms, the battlements of earlier periods being discontinued. A common layout at this period is the Z-plan, in which two wings or towers are set at diagonally opposite corners of the main block allowing all-round flanking fire, as at Ballone in the Highlands and Claypotts at Dundee. Walls were harled outside and plastered inside, and it was during this period that window glass replaced wooden shutters, carpets replaced rushes or straw, and furniture became less simple and sparse. The later castles have also a greater number of subdivisions at each level, giving more separate bedrooms, a kitchen and individual cellars for food, wine and other stores.

Many castles were involved in the troubles of the mid seventeenth century, but later most of them were either abandoned in favour of comfortable modern residences or were converted and extended, sometimes losing their original character. Many castles have now vanished through collapse and

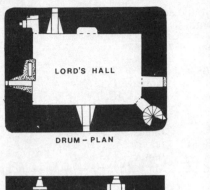

LORD'S HALL

DRUM – PLAN

DRUM – SECTION

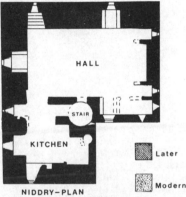

HALL

STAIR

KITCHEN

NIDDRY – PLAN

Later

Modern

0   5   10
METRES

HALL

KITCHEN

STAIR

LAW – PLAN

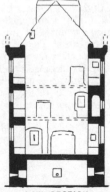

LAW – SECTION

Fig. 2. Early tower houses. Drum Castle (Gordon District) has a tower of about 1286 with vaults over three storeys while Law Castle (Cunninghame District) and Niddry Castle (West Lothian District) are less massive buildings of about 1467 and about 1500 respectively, with more sophisticated planning.

7

plundering for materials and the majority of those now surviving are in a state of utter ruin.

Monarchs of Scotland from 1057 to 1688

Malcolm III (Canmore) 1057-93
Donald II and Edmund 1093-7
Edgar 1097-1107
Alexander I 1107-24
David I 1124-53
Malcolm IV (The Maiden) 1153-65
William (The Lion) 1165-1214
Alexander II 1214-49
Alexander III 1249-86
Margaret (Maid of Norway) 1286-90
John Balliol 1292-6
Robert I (The Bruce) 1306-29
David II 1329-71

The Stewarts
Robert II 1371-90
Robert III 1390-1406
James I 1406-37
James II 1437-60
James III 1460-88
James IV 1488-1513
James V 1513-42
Mary 1542-67
James VI 1567-1625
Charles I 1625-49
Charles II 1650-85
James VII 1685-8

Public access to the castles

Ancient monuments maintained by the Scottish Office of Works are marked (AM) by the names. Standard opening hours are: April to September, 9.30 to 7.00 weekdays, 2.00 to 7.00 Sundays; October to March, 9.30 to 4.00 weekdays, 2.00 to 4.00 Sundays; some castles are now closed in winter. Ruins visitable free of charge at any reasonable time are additionally marked *.

National Trust properties are marked (NT) and private and corporately owned properties open to the public are marked (P). The Ordnance Survey grid reference of each castle is also given.

Buildings not specified as being ruined should be assumed to be private residences not normally open to the public. Most ruins can be inspected at the visitor's own risk although permission should be sought from landowners except where there is obvious public right of access.

Borders Region

Billie NT 851596

Only earthworks and the base of a massive keep or early tower house survive of a castle of the Dunbars, and later of the Earl of Angus. In 1540 it was granted to the Rentons but in 1544 it was one of many border castles destroyed by the Earl of Hertford in an attempt to force the Scots to betroth the infant Queen Mary to Henry VIII's son Edward.

Bite-About NT 794467

This very ruined L-plan pele house lies in a field.

Blanerne NT 832564

The ruined wing of an L-plan building and a structure called The Dairy, now hidden in trees behind a modern house, are all that remains of a Lumsdaine castle of about 1580-1610.

Borthwick NT 770544

The last traces of Patrick Cockburn's L-plan tower of about 1580-1610 were excavated before destruction by quarrying. There is now a commemorative stone near the site.

Bunkle NT 805596

The small fragments of masonry remaining at this large but overgrown Stewart castle of enclosure are undated.

Carfrae NT 506551

The small ruined tower house has a round stair turret.

Cockburnspath NT 785699

By a stream are a ruinous overgrown tower and outbuilding. They were probably built during James IV's reign, being assigned to his queen, and were later held by the Homes.

Cranshaws NT 681619

The Swintons' five-storey sixteenth-century tower passed to the Douglases in 1702 and became a home of Lord Aberdour.

Duns NT 777544

The L-plan tower of about 1500 was damaged by Hertford in 1544 and in 1639 was used as headquarters by General Leslie. It passed to the Hays of Drumelzier, who made considerable additions in the eighteenth and nineteenth centuries.

Edrington NT 943548

A fragment of the castle is incorporated in farm buildings.

Evelaw NT 661526
The ruin is a four-storey L-plan tower of about 1570-1600.

Fast NT 862710
Fast Castle stands on a coastal promontory. It was taken from the English in 1410 by a surprise attack by Patrick, son of the Earl of Dunbar. After destruction by Albany in 1515, the castle was rebuilt by the Homes in 1521. It fell to the English in the 1540s and, before recovery by a strategem in 1548, a plan of it was made which survives at Belvoir Castle and almost corresponds with the meagre remains. The castle was captured by Sir William Drury in 1570 on his way to Edinburgh. It passed in 1580 to the Logans of Restalrig and was probably abandoned after their forfeiture in 1600.

Greenknowe NT 639428 (AM*)
The ruined L-plan tower bears the date 1581 and the initials of J. Seton of Touch and his wife, J. Edmonstone. It was later purchased by the Pringles of Stichel.

Hirsel NT 829407 (P)
The nineteenth-century seat of the Earl of Home contains work of the seventeenth century and possibly earlier.

Home NT 704414
Fragments and foundations of the Homes' early courtyard castle are incorporated in a folly built about 1770 for the Earl of Marchmont. The castle was captured by the English in 1547 but recovered by Lord Home in 1549. It was battered into surrender by the Earl of Sussex in 1569, and by Colonel Fenwick for Cromwell in 1650, and then finally demolished.

Hutton NT 887548
In 1573 Elizabeth and Patrick Home added a substantial mansion on a stepped L-plan to an earlier sixteenth-century tower house with a round stair turret.

Leitholm NT 784438
In a field near Stainrig House is a very ruinous tower.

Nisbet NT 795512
Sir Alexander Nisbet's mansion of about 1610-20 has two round turrets on one side and two square turrets on the other.

Scarlaw NT 652564
One wall of a tower survives in a cottage by Watch Water.

Wedderlie NT 640515
The Edgars added a late seventeenth-century L-plan house to

their tiny late sixteenth-century L-plan tower, and in 1733 they sold the property to Lord Blantyre.

ETTRICK AND LAUDERDALE DISTRICT

Appletreeleaves NT 494366

The basement of the Darlings' tower on the slope of Blaikie's Hill is now in use as a storeroom.

Bemersyde NT 592334

The nucleus of the seat of the Haigs of Bemersyde is an early sixteenth-century tower house.

Blackhouse NT 281273

By the Douglas Burn is the basement of a tower of the Stewarts of Traquair with a round stair turret at a corner.

Buckholm NT 482378

This ruined tower in a corner of a barmkin beside a later house bears the date 1582 and the initials of John Pringle (or Hoppringle) and his wife. The Hoppringles held an earlier tower here for the English in 1547.

Colmslie NT 513396

The Cairncross family's ruined tower stands by a farmyard.

Corsbie NT 607438

Two sides stand high of the Cranstouns' tower in a marsh.

Cowdenknowes NT 579371

A small late tower house has been adapted to form the entrance hall of a modern mansion of the Earl of Home.

Cramalt NT 197227

Traces of two towers lie beneath the Megget Reservoir.

Crookston NT 425522

The seventeenth-century and later house includes a part of John Borthwick's tower house of about 1450.

Darnick NT 532343

This T-plan tower, with parapets and a watch chamber over the stair wing, bears the date 1569 and the initials of Andrew Heiton and his wife. There is a later extension. A ruinous second tower lies close by within the garden.

Deuchar NT 360280

Only the barest traces remain of the early sixteenth-century tower of the Homes, Murrays and finally the Dewars.

Dryhope NT 267247
Reset on a cartshed of a farm near the existing ruin is a stone from it with the date 1613 and the initials of Phillip and Mary Scott. A previous tower of Dickie of Dryhope was demolished in 1592 for his being 'art and parte in the late treasonable attempt against the King at Falkland'.

Eldinhope NT 305238
By the Eldinhope Burn is the base of a tower of the Scotts.

Elibank NT 397363
The ruined L-plan mansion was built in about 1600 by the lawyer Sir Gideon Murray. His son became Lord Elibank in 1643.

Ewes NT 434448
Only a heap of stones remains of a tower and a barmkin.

Fairnilee NT 458327
Part of the Kers' seventeenth-century mansion has been restored while the remainder has been destroyed to its base.

Gamescleugh NT 284147
Only the basement survives of Simon Scott's tower house.

Hillslap NT 513394
The L-plan tower bearing the date 1585 and the initials of N. Cairncross and his wife, EL, was restored in the 1980s.

Kirkhope NT 379250
This neglected tower was usually held by the eldest son of the Scott laird of Harden and was the home of the famous border reiver 'Auld Wat' when he was a young man courting the beautiful Mary Scott of Dryhope, celebrated in border ballads as the 'Flower of Yarrow'. They were married in 1576.

Langshaw NT 516397
Little remains of a late sixteenth-century L-plan tower, and the Murrays' later extension is also very ruinous.

Little Dean NT 633314
After being burnt in 1544, the thinly-walled rectangular pele house of a branch of the Kers of Cessford was given a substantial semi circular tower at one end with gunports.

Newark NT 421294
This very large ruined tower house was the 'New Werk' granted to Archibald, Earl of Douglas, in 1423. It was then

incomplete and work on it continued until about 1475, while the surrounding barmkin was added about 1550, and the present battlements and two square caphouses about 1600. The worn royal arms on the west gable are associated with James III's consort, Margaret of Denmark, who was granted the tower in 1473. Lord Grey unsuccessfully assaulted it in 1547, though it was burnt in 1548. In 1645 a hundred Royalist prisoners taken at the nearby battle of Philiphaugh were shot in the barmkin. Alterations were carried out for the widowed Anna, Duchess of Monmouth and Buccleuch, about 1690-1700.

Oakwood NT 420260
The existing tower bears the reset date 1602 and the initials of Robert Scott and L. Murray, although William Scott probably had a tower here in the 1540s.

Old Gala NT 492359
The mansion has a sixteenth-century pele house on the north-east and a T-plan building of 1611 in the middle.

Old Thirlestane NT 564474
A wing and one side remain of a sixteenth-century tower.

Rhymers NT 572383
Behind a garage near Earlston is part of a ruined tower.

Riddel NT 516245 and 520248
The ruined house of about 1700 and later has a dormer pediment of the 1560s. The nearby motte bears a tower of 1885.

Salenside NT 464207
The basement of a tower house has been removed.

Selkirk NT 470281
The motte and bailey north of Haining Loch are mentioned in the foundation charter of Selkirk Abbey of 1119. The timber buildings were rebuilt by Edward I in the 1300s.

Thirlestane NT 281154
Near a mansion is a ruined L-plan tower, which formerly had a lintel bearing the initials of Sir Robert Scott and his first wife, Margaret Cranstoun, whom he married in 1590.

Thirlestane NT 534479 (P)
James VI's faithful Chancellor Sir John Maitland, who died in office in 1595, built this remarkable castle. The main block has a round tower with a square caphouse at each corner and there are

on each side three round turrets carrying balustrades of later date. A seventeenth-century Duke of Lauderdale added the wings and there are other additions.

Torwoodlee NT 467378
The L-plan mansion replaced a tower sacked by the Elliots in 1568 and formerly had on it a stone with the year 1601 and the initials of George Pringle and his wife, MS.

Tushielaw NT 300172
Adam Scott was permitted to build a tower here in 1507. In 1530 he was executed for being the 'king of Theivis' and 'theftuously taking Blackmaill'. The base of his tower and a ruined outbuilding stand on a shelf above a road.

Whiteside NT 664384
Only the basement remains of this long narrow pele house.

Whitslaid NT 557446
The Lauders' ruined sixteenth-century tower was later given gables in replacement of the former open battlements.

Whytebank NT 442377
The remains of James Pringle's tower house and courtyard lie high up on the east slope of Knowes Hill.

Windydoors NT 432398
The base of the tower stands by a farm.

ROXBURGH DISTRICT

Allanmouth NT 455102
Only the vaulted basement of this tower house now survives.

Barnhills NT 589212
The basement of a tower burnt in 1545 lies in a field.

Bedrule NT 598180
Only the barest traces survive of an oval castle of enclosure with five round flanking towers, built in the thirteenth century by the Comyns and later held by the Turnbulls.

Branxholm NT 464116
The existing Z-plan castle with two small square towers and a courtyard was built by Sir Walter Scott to replace an older castle destroyed in 1570. Within it a doorway commemorates his death in 1574 and his widow's completion of the work in 1576. The Scotts were often Wardens of the Scottish Middle March and

were greatly involved both as lawkeepers and lawbreakers in the raiding and feuding that kept the borderland alight throughout the sixteenth century. A later Sir Walter Scott led the raid that rescued Kinmont Willie Armstrong from confinement in Carlisle Castle in 1596.

Burnhead NT 514166
Incorporated in a house are the lower parts of the tower of Hobbie Elliot, accused of making a foray in 1584.

Cavers NT 540154
The Balliols are thought to have had a stone castle of enclosure here, which in 1352-3 was given to William, Lord Douglas. However, the *castrum* mentioned in a charter of 1511 to James Douglas probably refers to the present ruined and much altered tower without any ancient features, and probably then newly built. It was burnt by Lord Dacre and Scott of Branxholm in 1542 and by Hertford in 1545, and it was later engulfed in a mansion destroyed in the 1930s.

Cessford NT 738238
This exceptionally massive L-plan tower close to the border was probably built by Andrew Ker soon after 1446. When the Earl of Surrey besieged it in 1523 with powerful cannon he reckoned it was the third strongest castle in Scotland and was grateful when the absent Ker laird arranged for it to be surrendered on generous terms. The tower was then dismantled and after restoration was damaged again by Hertford in 1545.

Chesterhouse NT 772203
Only the foundations remain of a tiny, thinly walled tower.

Corbet NT 776239
Above the Kale Water and in front of a mansion is a tiny tower house, much altered inside, which bears the date 1572 and the initials of John Ker and his wife, BI.

Crumhaugh NT 485138
A ruin survives of this tower.

Fairnington NT 646280
The wing of the seventeenth-century mansion incorporates the cellar of the 'bastell house' burnt by Hertford in 1544.

Fatlips NT 582209
In spite of restoration in 1897 as a shooting box and museum, the Turnbulls' tower on Minto Crags is now derelict.

Ferniehurst NT 652179

This castle, now a youth hostel, stands above the Jed Water near Jedburgh and was the seat of the Ker Warden on the Scottish Middle March. It was supposedly built about 1490 and was destroyed by Surrey in 1523. In 1549 it was captured by the French allies of the Scots and the English garrison was killed. The castle was burnt by the English in 1570, rebuilt and then demolished by James VI in 1593 because of Ker aid to the rebel Earl of Bothwell. The present castle has a long main block raised above the cellars of one range of a courtyard castle. It has one round tower and a high square wing, with the entrance and main stair, bearing the date 1598 and the initials of Andrew Ker. It has few defensive features.

Fulton NT 605158

Near the Rule Water is a ruined L-plan tower held in 1570 by Margaret Hume before her marriage to William Turnbull.

Goldielands NT 635226

Grose's view of 1789 shows that the Scotts' tower, now a ruin by a farm, once had a square courtyard with two turrets.

Hawick NT 499140 and 502144

South-west of the town is the Lovells' 25 foot (7.6 m) high motte. In the town itself is the Tower Hotel, a small L-plan tower which survived the burning of the town in 1570 and was much altered and extended for the Queensberry family in 1677.

Hermitage NY 497960 (AM)

This castle, restored externally but gutted inside, lies in a lonely position at the head of Liddesdale, a valley notorious for the lawlessness of its inhabitants. A thirteenth-century castle is probably represented by faint earthworks around the nearby chapel and was the place where Sir William Douglas starved Sir Alexander Ramsey to death in 1342. One of the English family of Dacre married Douglas's widow and built the core of the present castle as a fortified manor house with a pair of tenement blocks separated by a tiny court. The Douglases regained Hermitage in 1371 and remodelled it into a very large tower house with an entrance wing at one end. To it about 1400 were added three square corner towers and later a large kitchen wing was added to the other corner. Flying arches link the projections at each end. Within the four storeys were numerous rooms.

In 1492 the unreliable Douglas, Earl of Angus, was made to exchange castles with the Hepburns of Bothwell, who proved just as bad. In 1566 Patrick Hepburn, Earl of Bothwell, lay at Hermitage after being wounded in a border fray and was visited by Queen Mary, who, by riding the round journey of 50 miles (80 km) over rough moorland from Jedburgh and back in a day earned herself a fever and much scandal besides. With the attainder of the fifth Earl in 1594 Hermitage reverted to the Crown, although it was later held by the Scotts.

Jedburgh NT 647202 and 651206
The Gaol stands on the site of a motte. The T-plan Queen Mary's House is supposed to have accommodated her in 1566 when she came on a justice eyre suppressing border reivers. Nothing survives of two other former tower houses in the town.

Lanton NT 618215
The basement of a small tower is incorporated in a farm.

Liddel NY 510900
Ramparts dividing off inner and outer courts on a promontory remain of the timber castle of Ranulph de Soulis, where his nephew was murdered in 1207. Edward I was here in 1296.

Mangerton NY 479853
A ruined sixteenth-century tower house survives.

Mervinslaw NT 671117
This is the smallest and best preserved of a number of pele houses dating from about 1580 to about 1620 around the Jed Water. It was the home of the Olivers and had a single living room, without any amenities, set over a byre for cattle. Similar buildings are Northbank, Slacks, Overton and Dykeraw, while Clessy is now reduced to overgrown mounds. Foundations of Grey Coat lie 1100 feet (335 m) up several miles south of Hawick.

Roxburgh NT 713337
Founded by David I, Roxburgh Castle was classed as one of the chief strongholds in Scotland in 1174, when, along with Berwick, Edinburgh and Stirling, it was surrendered to the English after their capture of King William at Alnwick. It was destined to be often in English hands, with the Scots forever trying to get it back. In 1314 Sir James Douglas stormed the bailey, although the Gascon governor held the keep for another day. Henry V made repairs after a siege by the Scots in 1417. In 1460 James II was killed when one of the guns with which he was bombarding the castle blew up alongside him. His queen hurried to Roxburgh with the eight-year-old James III and had the castle stormed and demolished.

In 1545, on the recommendation of Hertford, the English built a roughly rectangular fort on the middle third of the site. It was demolished in 1550 under the terms of the Treaty of Boulogne, but a plan made in about 1548 has survived. Fragments remain on a long ridge by the Teviot near Kelso.

Slaidmills NT 429095
A ruined sixteenth-century tower house survives.

Smailholm NT 637346 (AM)
The Pringles' tower and barmkin on an outcrop of Lady Hill were attacked by the English in 1543, and again in 1546, when the garrison of Wark made off with sixty cattle and four prisoners. Like many of their neighbours, the family was forced to change its allegiance temporarily from Scotland to England in order to survive. In the 1580s the tower was given its unusual top vault with sections of open wall-walk on either side. It later passed to the Scotts of Harden.

Stirches NT 498162
This much altered and extended tower of the Scotts was originally called Stirkshaw. It was sold to Walter Chisholm in 1650 and bears the initials of his son William and his wife, Mary Brotherston of Glencairn, with the date 1686.

Timpendean NT 636226
The ruined sixteenth-century four-storey tower of the Douglases stands within an earlier earthwork enclosure.

Wallace's NT 700304
By the Tweed near Roxburgh is a ruined and overgrown tower with wings at two corners. It was granted to Walter and Isobel Ker of Cessford in 1543.

Whitclaugh NY 488880
The basement of a tower survives in the modern mansion.

Whitton NT 759222
John Riddel built his now ruined tower after receiving a charter in 1602. It replaced a tower destroyed in 1523.

TWEEDDALE DISTRICT

Barns NT 215391
The empty tower on an eminence by the house has initials of William Burnet and Margaret Stewart, who married in 1576.

Black Barony NT 236472
Sir Alexander Murray's symmetrical house of about 1700-15 incorporates a sixteenth-century L-plan tower house.

Cardrona NT 300378
On the side of Cardrona Hill is a ruined L-plan tower built by the Govans and later held by the Williamsons.

Castlehill NT 214354
The ruined fifteenth-century tower of the Lowis family of Manor stands on a knoll by the Manor Water.

Chapelhill NT 245421
The farmhouse is a much altered tower of the Pringles.

Colquhar NT 332416
By the junction of the Leithen Water and Hope Burn are the last remains of a Ker tower later held by the Morrisons.

Drochil NT 162434
This unusual ruined Z-plan castle, with two round flanking towers set at diagonally opposite corners of a central block with a central corridor at each storey, was built by the Douglas Earl of Morton, an effective but unpopular ruler of Scotland as Regent from 1572 to 1578. Drochil was unfinished when in 1581 he was executed on a charge of complicity in the murder of James VI's father, Lord Darnley, in 1567.

Drumelzier NT 124334
The ruins of this castle of the Tweedies, which passed in 1632 to John, Lord Hay of Yester, comprise an added sixteenth-century wing with a square tower on the outer corner.

Easter Deans NT 226532
The farmhouse incorporates part of a tower of the Ramseys.

Eddleston NT 243472
Moredun House, west of Eddleston church, incorporates the much altered lower part of a small tower house.

Flemington NT 166451
The small and altered tower of the Hays, and later the Veitches, stands among the outbuildings of a farmhouse.

Glentress NT 342432
By the Glentress Burn is the almost buried base of a tower.

Haystoun NT 259383
The nucleus of the Hays' house is an L-plan building of the late sixteenth or early seventeenth century.

Horsburgh NT 285391
The small ruined L-plan tower of the Horsburgh family stands on a mound by the Tweed below Peebles.

Hutchinfield NT 255422
Only the lower part of the Horsburghs' tower survives.

Langhaugh NT 202310
In 1561 Janet Scott, widow of John Baird of Posso, had difficulty in recovering the tower from the tenant, William Cockburn. Only the almost buried foundations remain.

Laur NT 179356
The foundations stand on a hill high above Stobo church.

Lee NT 328396
By a farm is a small ruined tower formerly occupied by tenants of the Homes and later the Kers.

Manorhead NT 195276
The basement of the tower of the Inglises stands in a farmyard.

Neidpath NT 236404 (P)
Above the Tweed near Peebles is the large late fourteenth-century L-plan tower house of the Hays, created Earls of Tweeddale in the seventeenth century. The tower is much altered inside and has courtyard buildings of the sixteenth and seventeenth centuries on the side away from the river.

Nether Horsburgh NT 304396
There are ruins of a sixteenth-century tower and court of the Horsburghs, sold in the seventeenth century because of financial difficulties to Sir Robert Stewart of Shillingshaw.

Peebles NT 249403
This motte is probably where Henry, Earl of Huntingdon, son of David I, died in 1152. The castle was garrisoned for Edward I in 1301-2 and remained in use until at least 1334.

Plora NT 359360
Above the Plora Burn are scanty traces of the tower and courtyard of the Lowis family.

Posso NT 200332
There are scanty traces of the tower of the Bairds, and later of the Naesmiths, and a ruin of one of the outbuildings.

Purvishill NT 355375
Built into a field dyke are scanty remnants of a tower.

St Gordians NT 194307
A supposed chapel is now known to be the remains of a tower.

Shieldgreen NT 273432
The remains of a tower have a rock-cut ditch on one side.

Skirling NT 072398
The Cockburns' moated castle of enclosure was blown up in 1568 by the Regent Moray because they supported Queen Mary. Only the moat remains but excavation revealed foundations.

Tinnies NT 141344
The Tweedies' small castle of about 1500 with a tower house on one side and two round flanking towers on the other is very ruinous. It was supposedly blown up by the son of John, Lord Fleming, whom the Tweedies murdered in 1524, causing a feud.

Traquair NT 330354 (P)
The present mansion of the Maxwell Stuarts contains work of all periods added to a sixteenth-century L-plan building lying on the site of an early royal hunting lodge.

West Linton NT 149519
The small L-plan tower of the Melrose family was extended in the eighteenth century and altered more recently.

Whitslade NT 112350
Near the house is the basement of a tower held in turn by the Porteouses, the Murrays of Stanhope and the Dicksons.

Winkston NT 245430
Behind the farmhouse is a tower dated 1545 built by William Dickson and later altered by other families.

Woolandslee NT 317448
By the Woolandslee Burn at about 1000 feet (305 m) up is the basement of a small tower and traces of an outbuilding.

Wrae NT 115332
Only the stair turret remains of this tower of the Tweedies.

Central Region
CLACKMANNAN AND FALKIRK DISTRICTS

Airth NS 900868

An English pele on this site was captured by Wallace in 1297, and the castle was burnt by James III shortly before his murder in 1488. The frontage of the hotel is of 1807 but behind are a tower house of about 1490 and additions of the early sixteenth century and 1581 forming an L-plan.

Alloa NS 889925

The large but somewhat altered tower house with five large bartizans was built about 1360-80 by Sir Robert Erskine, Great Chamberlain under David II. It still belongs to the Erskine Earl of Mar and Kellie but is now empty. In it was born 'Bobbing John', the Earl of Mar who led the 1715 rising.

Almond NS 956773

In 1540 the Crawfords' large fifteenth-century L-plan tower and a more recent surrounding barmkin wall, now very ruinous, were acquired by the Livingstones, who later added apartments with square projecting bays on the south-east. The name was changed from Haining to Almond in 1633 when the Earl of Linlithgow's son James was created a baron. It was forfeited by the Livingstone Earl of Callendar in 1716.

Castle Campbell NS 962994 (AM)

Colin Campbell, a leading statesman of his day, created Earl of Argyll in 1457, built a tower on this beautifully sited promontory. He had the name changed from Castle Gloom to Castle Campbell in 1490 and died in 1493. Later Earls added a courtyard with buildings on all sides, now mostly ruined. The second Earl was killed at Flodden in 1513. The fourth Earl took a leading part in the battle of Pinkie in 1547 and at the siege of Haddington in 1548. He was the first Scottish noble to adopt Protestantism and in 1556 was probably host at Castle Campbell to the preacher John Knox.

Montrose defeated the prominent Covenanter Archibald, eighth Earl and first Marquis of Argyll, at Inverlochy and Kilsyth in 1645 but did not capture Castle Campbell. Argyll lived at the castle until Cromwell's forces occupied it in 1653. Only part was restored after a burning by Monck in 1654.

Castle Cary NS 786775

Among trees above the Red Burn is a late fifteenth-century tower and a lower extension dated 1679, screening a small court on the promontory behind. The yett from the tower is now reset within the extension. The castle was a seat of the Baillies and was burnt by the Jacobites in 1715.

Clackmannan NN 905920 (AM)
The late fourteenth-century tower on a hill above the town was begun by Robert Bruce, the son of a natural son of King Robert I. The tower was remodelled in the fifteenth century, being given a wing and a machicolated parapet. The last Bruce to inhabit the tower was a lady who knighted Robert Burns ceremoniously with her ancestor's sword.

Dunmore NS 890889
The cellar of the Elphinstones' sixteenth-century tower house has been the burial vault of the Earls of Dunmore since 1820. The altered superstructure is now very ruinous.

Herbertshire NS 804830
This large, altered and extended fifteenth-century L-plan tower is now known only from old drawings, having been demolished. It passed from the Sinclairs to Alexander, first Earl of Linlithgow, in 1608. It was later held by the Stirlings, who sold it to William Morehead in 1768.

Menstrie NS 852968
Only one range, now in a housing estate, survives from a courtyard house of the seventeenth century. It was the birthplace of Sir William Alexander, Earl of Stirling and coloniser of Nova Scotia, and in 1645 was damaged by Montrose.

Sauchie NS 896957
James Shaw's tower of about 1430-40 is a fine ruin with mural chambers, the entrance and the stair in a thick side wall.

Skaithmore NS 888834
The tower bears the date 1607 and the initials of Alexander, fourth Lord Elphinstone, Treasurer of Scotland, and Dame Jane Livingstone. It was later adapted for use as a coal pit pumping station and now lies gutted and forlorn.

Stenhouse NS 879829
In the 1960s the Carron Ironworks Company demolished this neglected and extended L-plan house dated 1622, with the initials of William Bruce and his second wife, Rachel Johnstone.

Torwoodhead NS 836844
This ruined L-plan house with shotholes was built about 1590 by the Baillies of Castle Cary, keepers of a royal forest here, and from 1635 Lords Forester of Corstorphine.

STIRLING DISTRICT

Arnhall NS 764986
On the Keir estate are ruins of a late L-plan building.

Balglass NS 585876
All that remains is revetments on the sides of a knoll and a stone with the date 1602 and the initials of M. Stirling reset on the adjacent farmhouse. It later passed to the Bontines, one of whom in 1648 murdered the Reverend John Collins, Presbyterian minister of Campsie.

Blairlogie NS 827969
Alexander Spittal's small tower of 1543, now called The Blair, stands by a burn above the village. Adam Spittal added a wing in 1582 and there are more recent extensions.

Bruce's NS 857878
This ruined tower was built in the fifteenth century probably by Sir William de Earth of Plean. It passed in about 1480 to Alexander Hepburn and was damaged in a family quarrel. It then went to the Bruces, who in 1512 were licensed to refortify it. In 1608 it went to the Drummonds of Carnock House, who changed the name from Carnock Tower to Bruce's Castle to distinguish between the two.

Callander NN 629076
Reset above the manse doorway is a stone from the destroyed castle with the date 1596 and the initials of Alexander Livingstone, first Earl of Linlithgow, and Lady Elizabeth Hay, tutors here to James VI's daughter Elizabeth.

Cardross NS 605976
The core of the eighteenth-century mansion is the Erskines' sixteenth-century tower with a round stair turret.

Coldoch NS 699982
The Spittals' tower lies amidst the Grahams' mansion.

Craigievern NS 495902
On a strong site by the Altquhur Burn are traces of a thick wall enclosing an area about 75 feet (23 m) in diameter.

Craigmaddie NS 575765
Near the house is the lower part of a tower built by the Hamiltons before they removed to Bardowie Castle by 1566.

Culcreuch NS 620876
The Galbraiths' sixteenth-century tower forms the south-west

corner of the house. A late eighteenth-century wing has a reset panel with the year 1721 and John Napier's initials.

Doune NN 728011

On a peninsula above the Teith and the Ardoch is the fine castle built about 1390-1400 by Robert, Duke of Albany, Regent of Scotland during the reign of his crippled elder brother, Robert III (christened John). It is one of the few large castles in Scotland to have been built in one campaign and has survived almost intact without notable later alterations. The courtyard has high walls on three sides and on the other a hall block with at one end a self-contained tower house with the gateway and its surviving original yett below it.

After Robert III's death in 1406 Albany continued to rule in the place of the young James I, then a prisoner in England. Albany's son Murdoch succeeded him as regent in 1420 but James returned in 1424 and soon had him executed. Doune was retained as a royal hunting lodge, state prison and dower house for the widows of James III, IV and V. It was occasionally used by Queen Mary, the suite of rooms over the kitchen being known as her apartments. In 1570 her forces gave up the castle to Regent Lennox after a short siege.

James VI was fond of Doune Castle, which was kept for him by the Stewart Lord Doune, created Earl of Moray in 1592. In 1593 the King surprised at the castle the Earls of Atholl, Montrose and Gowrie, who were plotting against him, the two latter being captured. It was occupied by Montrose in 1645 and by government troops in 1689 and 1715. The decayed castle was seized by the Jacobites in 1745 and used as a prison. It was restored from ruin in the late nineteenth century.

Duchray NS 480998

William Graham's tower house of about 1580-1600, with a round stair turret, was remodelled about 1825. Here in 1653 the Earl of Glencairn raised a Royalist force that defeated the Cromwellians at Aberfoyle. In the 1690s two Graham sisters entertained dragoon officers at the front while the celebrated Rob Roy Macgregor was smuggled out of the back.

Duke Murdoch's NN 473014

The scanty ruins of a small tower by Loch Ard are supposed to have been a hunting lodge of Murdoch, Duke of Albany.

Duntreath NS 536811

The late fifteenth-century tower house, still owned by the Edmonstones, who built it, adjoins the remains of a fourteenth-century hall of the Lennoxes. The castle was later developed with buildings around three sides of a court, with a gatehouse on the fourth, but these parts were demolished after a long period of neglect while the family was living in Ireland.

Edinample NN 601226
The somewhat altered and extended sixteenth-century Z-plan castle of Campbell of Breadalbane is to be restored in the 1980s. One of the round towers contains a bottle dungeon.

Finlarig NN 575338
Hidden in trees at the west end of Loch Tay is a Z-plan castle with two square towers built by Sir Colin Campbell of Glenorchy. A panel over the entrance has the date 1609 and the arms and initials of James VI and his queen.

Fintry NS 641863
The Graham castle of the fifteenth and sixteenth centuries, with a main block set on a knoll and with a wing or tower and a court to the north-east, was a ruin by 1724 and little survives.

Gargunnock NS 715944
A pele here was captured by Wallace. The nucleus of the present house is the Setons' sixteenth-century L-plan tower. The Erskine Earl of Mar added a wing after 1624.

Gartincaber NN 698000
The late seventeenth-century mansion has an older nucleus.

Gartmore NS 530978
Malcolm Macfarlane's late sixteenth-century Z-plan castle with two round towers lies ruinous near a Graham mansion.

Glorat NS 641779
The Stirlings' mansion has an early tower as its nucleus.

Graham's NS 662858
Only the moat remains of the pele of Sir John Graham, killed fighting alongside Wallace at Falkirk. The fragments of masonry nearby are of an outer court of a much later house.

Keir NN 770989
The mansion of the Stirlings, owners since 1448, is a composite building of many periods with a tower as the nucleus.

Kilbryde NN 756036
Nothing remains of Sir James Graham's castle of 1460, and the large L-plan building forming the nucleus of the house is only of the seventeenth century. It was sold in 1669 to Sir Colin Campbell of Aberuchill, Lord Justice Clerk.

Lanrick NN 685031
The tower of the Haldanes of Gleneagles was later the seat of the chief of the Macgregors. In 1840 the tea tycoon William Jardine incorporated it into a large new mansion.

Leckie NS 690946
The late sixteenth-century T-plan fortalice of David Muir now stands empty by a later mansion used as an eventide home.

Leny NS 613089
The nucleus of the house, now a hotel, is an L-plan sixteenth-century castle of the Buchanans.

Manor NS 827948
Little remains of a T-plan building formerly dated 1572 with the initials of Robert Callander. It was entire in 1850.

Menteith NN 572004
Doune Castle superseded the Earls of Menteith's residence on Inch Tulla, although it was occasionally used until about 1700. A hall and other humble ruined buildings surround a court.

Mugdock NN 549772
Mugdock was the home of the famous Graham Marquis of Montrose. It was spoiled by Lord Sinclair while Montrose was imprisoned at Edinburgh in 1641 and taken over by the Marquis of Argyll after Montrose was executed in 1650. It was returned to the Grahams when in 1661 Argyll in turn was executed. Surrounding John Guthrie Smith's ruined house of 1875 are remains of an inner court of about 1380-1400 with square corner towers. To the west is a large fifteenth-century outer court with later ruined outbuildings.

Newton Doune NN 731013
The Edmonstones' sixteenth-century L-plan tower has an unusual rounded gable on the wing.

Old Sauchie NS 779883
The Erskines' late sixteenth-century tower is a ruin but the adjoining later office range is still in use.

Plean NS 849869
A range and court were added in the sixteenth century to the Somervilles' small tower of about 1490 on a knoll. It was sold in 1634 to Thomas Nicolson and was later held by the Elphinstones. Restored about 1900, it is now ruined again.

Rednock NN 600022
A ruined turret of a Graham tower house lies by a farm.

Steuarthall NS 828929

This tower of about 1600-20, with a round stair turret and the initials of Sir Alexander Stirling and Anna Hamilton, was formerly called Wester Polmaise. There is a later east wing.

Stirling NS 790940

A fortress and palace on this volcanic rock are first known in the time of Alexander I, who built a chapel and died here in 1124. It came to prominence with the Wars of Independence, for it guarded the fords over the Forth. It changed hands several times before the famous siege of 1304, when, after the Scottish garrison submitted, Edward I made them stay inside until the castle had been struck by his novel and still untried siege engine the 'War Wolf'. The English held Stirling until the defeat at Bannockburn nearby in 1314 when attempting to relieve it. The garrison then yielded and the castle was destroyed, only to be rebuilt by Edward III after the victory of Halidon Hill in support of Edward Balliol. His garrison, besieged in 1337 by Sir Andrew de Moray, was relieved, but the Scots recovered the castle in 1342. Nothing is known of the nature of the defences and buildings during this period and the earliest part now surviving is the late fourteenth-century gateway below the Mint.

During his minority James II lived at Stirling under the care of Sir Alexander Livingstone until a rival, Sir William Crichton, carried the young king off to Edinburgh. James III was born in the castle in 1451 and had work begun on a fine new hall although most of it is the work of James IV about 1500. The truncated great forework enclosing the main palace yard on the vulnerable townward side is of the same period and comprises a curtain wall with a gatehouse in the middle with round corner towers and a rectangular tower at either end. James V built a palace famous for its Renaissance-influenced facades and with a court in the middle called the Lyon's Den.

James VI had the Chapel Royal rebuilt for the christening of his eldest son, Frederick Henry, in 1594, but Stirling lost its importance with his removal to London in 1603. It was refurbished for a brief visit by Charles I in 1633 and in 1651 was besieged by General Monck for Cromwell. It yielded after a few days because of a mutiny in the garrison. Most of the parapets overlooking the cliffs and the complex outer defences towards the town date from the time of Queen Anne and bear her monogram. A loyal garrison in the castle caused problems for the Jacobites in both the 1715 and 1745 revolts.

Touch NS 753928

The mansion of the Setons comprises a tower of about 1500, a long seventeenth-century range and a Georgian front.

Dumfries and Galloway Region

Annan NY 192668

The de Brus motte and bailey lie by the river Annan. A church tower used as a munitions store by the English in 1299 was captured and destroyed by them in 1547. The tower house of Lord Herries, which replaced it, has also now gone.

Auchen NT 063035

Above the former Beattock station are the ruins of a thirteenth-century castle of enclosure with massive walls and round turrets. The Earls of Moray and Morton held it in the fourteenth century, and the Maitlands in the fifteenth.

Auchenrivock NY 373805

This ruined Irvine tower was originally called Stakeheugh. It or a predecessor was burnt in 1513 by Christopher Dacre.

Barntalloch NY 353878

The motte and bailey have indications of later masonry.

Blacklaw NT 052067

By a barn is a ruined sixteenth-century Johnstone tower.

Blackwood (or Blacket) NY 243743

William Bell's ruined late sixteenth-century tower has stones with the dates 1663 and 1714 and the initials respectively of John and George Bell and their wives.

Bonshaw NY 243721

Thomas Irving's tower was burnt by the English in 1544. In 1585 it was twice besieged by Lord Maxwell, who became a prisoner in it in 1586 after his capture by the Johnstones.

Breconside NT 109022

This Johnstone tower near Moffat is now part of a farm.

Cornal NT 112044

By the Cornal Burn is a fragment of a sixteenth-century tower of the Carruthers family, and later of the Douglases.

Frenchland NT 102054

The late sixteenth-century tower is named after Robert Frenchie, who built it. The stair wing is an addition.

Gilnockie (or Hollows) NY 383787

The tower of Johnnie Armstrong, one of a family renowned

29

for lawless exploits on both sides of the border throughout the sixteenth century, was restored and reoccupied by a descendant in the 1970s. James V set an example to the unruly inhabitants of Liddesdale in 1530 by hanging without trial a number of Armstrongs, Johnnie among them. The tower was later rebuilt at the top and given a beacon-fire stance on one gable after being damaged by the English.

Hoddom NY 157730

John Maxwell's massive L-plan tower of about 1560 was surrendered to the Regent Moray in 1568 after a siege of only a day. Moray installed in it Douglas of Drumlanrig, his Warden of the Scottish West March, but in 1569 it was recaptured by Queen Mary's forces and in 1570 was blown up by the English. Restored, the tower was obtained in 1627 by Richard Murray from the sixth Lord Herries and the wing was then heightened. Hoddom passed to the Earl of Southesk in 1653, to the Sharps in 1690 and later to the Brookes.

Langholm NY 361849 and 365855

The tower which was betrayed to the English in 1544 was probably the ruin lying in a field between the two rivers. The cellar of a second tower survives in the base of a wing of the Buccleuch Arms Hotel in the main street.

Lochhouse NT 082034

The tower belonged to the Johnstones of Corehead.

Lochmaben NY 082822 and 088812 (AM*)

About 1298 Edward I replaced the de Brus motte by the town with a pele, with inner and outer enclosures in line, on a peninsula on the south side of the loch. Edward III in the 1360s had the inner court surrounded by very thick walls.

Lochwood NY 085968

Adjoining a motte are traces of the L-plan tower and court seized by the English in 1547. All the historical records of the Johnstone Earls of Annandale were lost in 1585 when the castle was burnt by Robert Maxwell and the Armstrongs.

Lockerbie NY 136816

The now destroyed tower was one of two Johnstone houses in Lockerbie captured in 1582 by the Earl of Morton. In 1593 Mungo Johnstone's house was attacked by Lord Maxwell, who was killed when Johnstone raised the siege. The tower was reduced in height later when used as a prison.

Lunelly NY 193821

Only a fragment of this Johnstone tower now survives.

Mellingshaw NT 038087
Part of the Johnstones' tower survives.

Raecleugh NT 038118
The sixteenth-century Johnstone tower is now a ruin.

Repentance NY 155723
This odd little late sixteenth-century tower was a lookout point for Hoddom Castle on lower ground nearby.

Robgill NY 248716
In a mansion is the basement of Cuthbert Irving's tower, burnt by the English in 1544, and held for them in 1547.

Spedlins NY 098877
The lower part of the Jardines' tower is of the fifteenth century and the gabled upper part with bartizans is of 1605.

Stapleton NY 234688
Fergus Graham's rebuilt and now gutted tower was captured in 1626 by a surprise attack by Christie Irving.

Woodhouse NY 251715
The Irvings' sixteenth-century tower house lies in ruins.

NITHSDALE DISTRICT

Abbot's Tower NX 972666
This ruined L-plan tower near a farm was built about 1550 by John Broun, penultimate abbot of nearby Sweetheart Abbey.

Amisfield NX 992838
By a mansion is an empty tower dated 1600 with the arms and initials of John Charteris and Agnes Maxwell.

Barjarg NX 876901
The L-plan tower was probably built after 1587 by Thomas Grierson. Nearby is a stone with the date 1603 and the Maxwell arms and on an extension are the date 1680 and the initials of John Grierson and Grissel Kirkpatrick.

Bogrie NX 812849
The Kirkoes' sixteenth-century tower was lowered and made into a house in 1860. It bears the date 1660 with the initials of John Kirkoe and Jean Maxwell, while another stone with the year 1770 refers to a period of Gordon tenure.

Breckonside NX 841889
Only the base remains of this small Maxwell tower house.

Caerlaverock NY 026656 and 027655 (AM)

In 1300 the newly built castle suffered a famous siege by Edward I, described in a contemporary poem referring to it as being triangular with a tower at each of two corners with a twin-towered gatehouse at the third. Though much of the present walling is of later date the castle still retains this basic shape and is surrounded by a broad wet moat. The castle was dismantled about 1310-12 by the Bruces and later a rectangular new castle was begun in the marshes nearer the sea, where a moat and buried foundations remain. The original castle was patched up before 1400 by the Maxwells and became their chief seat. They were forced to surrender it peacefully to the English in 1544, and though recovered by them it was recaptured and dismantled by the Earl of Essex in 1570. Patched up again, the castle was remodelled by Robert, Lord Maxwell, created Earl of Nithsdale in 1620. He added the very fine set of apartments on the east and south sides with magnificent facades with classical details towards the tiny court. The castle was in 1640 captured and finally destroyed by the Covenanters.

Closeburn NX 907921

The fourteenth-century tower is intact and little altered.

Comlongon NY 079690

The substantial fifteenth-century tower with a yett still surviving was built by the Murrays to replace the vanished nearby castle of Cockpool. It stands empty beside the mansion of their descendant the Earl of Mansfield.

Cowhill NX 952806

The L-plan tower, bearing the date 1597 and the initials of Robert and Barbara Maxwell, was partly demolished in 1789.

Cullochan NX 920755

The foundations of a tower stand on a motte created out of a spur rising high above the north bank of the Cargen Water.

Dalswinton NX 945841

In the estate is the almost buried vaulted basement of a tower with a round stair turret still standing high.

Dumfries NX 975754

The twelfth-century royal castle was one of four mottes in the area guarding the Nith. It was seized by Robert Bruce in 1296 and was held by the English until 1306, when the more famous Robert Bruce, grandson of the former, stormed it immediately after his killing of John Comyn in the Franciscan church here. The castle was retaken by the Macdoualls in 1307 but was finally captured and demolished in 1313.

Elliock NS 796074
The house incorporates part of the fortalice sold by the Crichtons to James Stewart in 1593 and later held by the Dalziels.

Elshieshields NY 069850
In 1602 Wilkin Johnstone's house of 'Elsiechellis' was burned by Maxwell of Kirkhouse. The L-plan tower by the Ae Water has bartizans and a stance for a warning beacon fire.

Enoch NS 879009
By the Carron Burn are buried foundations of a tower.

Fourmerkland NX 909807
The tower has bartizans at opposite corners and has the date 1590 with the initials of Robert Maxwell and his wife.

Isle NX 955825
The small tower beside the Nith with diagonally opposite bartizans and a surviving yett bears the date 1587 and the initials of John Fergusson and his wife, BR.

Isle NY 028689
Near Bankend is a small, shattered T-plan tower once dated 1622 with the initials of Edward Maxwell and Helen Douglas.

Kirkconnel NX 979697
The mid sixteenth-century L-plan tower of the Maxwells was altered by James Maxwell in 1780, on his return from exile after the 1745 Jacobite rebellion, and has been extended.

Lag NX 880862
The Griersons' small ruined tower stands on a mound.

Morton NX 891992
The castle consists of a ruined hall block with a tower at one end and a gatehouse at the other, being set across the neck of a promontory above Castle Loch. It was built by the Douglas Earl of Morton about 1440-50 and in 1459 passed to a junior branch of the family.

Mousewald NY 051739
The ruin of a tower adjoins Mousewald Place.

Old Crawfordton NX 815889
The ruin by a farm belonged to John Crichton in 1656.

Portrack NX 935832
Near Portrack House is a fragment of a Maxwell tower.

Sanquhar NS 795093

The Crichtons' ruined castle stands near the town. The seventeenth-century outer courtyard wall is reduced to its foundations but more survives of the fifteenth-century inner court with a keep-gatehouse and apartments, and a square corner tower survives from a courtyard castle of about 1370-1400. William Crichton, created Earl of Dumfries in 1630, sold Sanquhar to Sir William Douglas, newly created Earl of Queensberry. The third Earl and first Duke of Queensberry retired from public life in 1685 and built himself a very fine new quadrangular mansion at Drumlanrig a few miles away. However, he continued to reside, and died, at Sanquhar Castle, which was finally abandoned only by his successor.

Sundaywell NX 811845

Parts of a sixteenth-century tower remain in the farmhouse. A reset stone is dated 1651 with the initials of John Kirkoe.

Tibbers NX 863983

In the Drumlanrig estate are the overgrown ruins of a rectangular courtyard with round corner towers and a twin-towered gatehouse begun in 1298 by Richard Siward, a Scot created Sheriff of Dumfries by Edward I. Bruce captured it in 1306 and on its recapture Edward had the governor, John de Seton, hanged. It was later held by the Earl of March and in 1489 went to the Maitland family.

Torthorwald NY 033783

The massive ruined fourteenth-century tower of the Carlyles, created peers about 1475, stands within probably earlier earthworks. It later passed to the Douglas family.

Wreath's NX 953565

Only a fragment survives of a sixteenth-century tower held by the Douglas Regent Morton, and later by the Maxwells.

STEWARTRY DISTRICT

Auchenskeoch NX 917588

At Castle Farm are a round corner tower and some walling.

Balmangan NX 651456

Adjoining the house is the basement of a tower house.

Barclosh NX 855624

A fragment of a tower stands near Barclosh farmhouse.

Buittle NX 899616 and 897616

Among trees and undergrowth by the Urr are remains of the

twin-towered gateway of a thirteenth-century castle of enclosure built for Dervorguilla of Galloway and her husband, John Balliol, a powerful English baron. Their son, born at Buittle in 1267, was John Balliol, chosen in 1292 by Edward I of England to be King of Scots after the failure of the male line of Malcolm Canmore. John was nicknamed Toom Tabard (empty coat) for his lack of spirit and when he did try to resist the domineering English king he was summarily deposed in 1296. He died in exile in France, although his son Edward returned to usurp David II briefly in the 1330s. However, Buittle Castle was not restored after destruction by the Bruces about 1312. In the late sixteenth century it was superseded by a nearby L-plan tower house called Buittle Place. This was ruinous in the eighteenth century but was restored in the nineteenth, when the bartizans were removed.

Cally NX 598554
A fragment of a tower lies hidden in bushes near the hotel.

Cardoness NX 591552 (AM)
This impressive tower on a rock overlooking the mouth of the Fleet was erected by the M'Cullochs about 1480-1510. Only the lowest parts remain of later courtyard walls and buildings. The second M'Culloch laird was outlawed in 1471 and again in 1480, while in 1690 Sir Godfrey M'Culloch shot Gordon of Bush o'Bield, then owner, at his own front door and was executed for it on return from exile.

Corra NX 867662
Half of a low, late building lies in ruins by a farm.

Cumstoun NX 683533
Half of a tower of about 1500-30 stands above the modern house.

Drumcoltran NX 869684
The now empty L-plan tower was probably built for Sir John Maxwell after his marriage in 1550 to Agnes, heiress of Lord Herries. It passed in 1668 to the Irvines, who carried out minor alterations, and was later held by the Hynds and the Herons, before reverting to the Maxwells of Terregles.

Dundeugh NX 602880
Hidden among trees and undergrowth are the last remains of a tiny sixteenth-century L-plan tower and an outbuilding.

Earlstoun NX 613840
The Sinclairs' L-plan sixteenth-century tower is now only a store. Reset on it, from a now destroyed east extension, is a

stone with the year 1655 and the initials of William Gordon and Mary Hope. Although intended for the church, William ended up as a soldier, being killed at Bothwell Bridge in 1679. Earlstoun was subsequently occupied by troops engaged in suppressing the Covenanters.

Edingham NX 839626
The low ruined tower in a field dates from about 1600.

Hills NX 912726
The tower was built shortly after 1527 and bears the arms of Edward Maxwell and Janet Carson. The house on the east is dated 1721 and has reset stones of John Maxwell, Lord Herries, and Edward and Agnes Maxwell. About 1600 the latter pair had built the charming little gateway to the small barmkin.

Kenmure NX 635764
The early lords of Galloway are said to have had a strong-hold on this fine site by Loch Ken. It was aquired by the Gordons of Lochinvar in 1297. They became Viscounts Kenmure in the 1630s. The castle was burnt in 1568 after Queen Mary's defeat at Langside, and again in 1650 by Cromwell's forces. The existing L-planned building has part of a tower house of about 1570-1600 and the remainder dates from several periods in the seventeenth century, with alterations of the nineteenth, when it was restored from ruin. After a fire in the early twentieth century the castle is now ruinous again.

Kirkcudbright NX 677508
Only the moat survives of Alexander III's castle destroyed by the Bruces and never restored. Excavations in 1911-13 showed that there was a small rectangular court with a twin round-towered gatehouse at one end and a pair of large round corner towers at the other end, one being a keep.

Lochinvar NX 656853
On an islet, the base of a large tower with a round stair turret remains of the seat of the Gordons of Lochinvar.

Maclellans NX 683511 (AM)
Within Kirkcudbright is a large L-planned mansion bearing the date 1582 and the arms of Sir Thomas Maclellan of Bombie and Dame Grissel Maxwell. The Maclellans were impoverished by involvement in the Civil Wars and the house has been roofless since about 1752, when it passed to Robert Maxwell of Orchardton, who in turn sold it to the Earl of Selkirk in 1782.

Orchardton NX 817551 (AM*)
The tower house of John Carnys of about 1450 is unique in

Scotland, being round both externally and internally, save for the roughly rectangular vaulted cellar, without access to the upper rooms. There is a tiny later court and outbuildings.

Plunton NX 605507
The large triangular moat probably enclosed a wooden house of the M'ghies. Within it is a ruined L-plan tower built by the Lennox family in the late sixteenth century.

Rusko NX 584605
Below the B796 is a tower built by Robert Gordon after marriage to the heiress of Sir Robert Ackerson, and before he succeeded as laird of Lochinvar in 1513. Little remains of a later extension but the tower was restored in the 1970s.

Shirmers NX 657743
By the farm is a low fragment of a sixteenth-century Gordon tower. It or a predecessor was burnt in 1568.

Threave NX 739623 (AM)
On one side of a 20 acre (8 ha) island in the river Dee is the mighty tower house built by Archibald the Grim, Lord of Galloway from 1369 onwards, Earl of Wigtown after 1372, and Earl of Douglas from 1388 until his death at Threave in 1400. It was he who restored order in unruly Galloway. His son Archibald served with the French and was created Duke of Touraine, being killed at Verneuil in 1424, after which his widow, James I's sister Margaret, ruled Galloway from Threave until about 1450. The Black Douglases became the most powerful family in Scotland and incurred the jealousy and mistrust of James II. During the King's minority the young sixth Earl and his brother were murdered in 1440 by the Regents Livingstone and Crichton in the 'Black dinner' at Edinburgh Castle. In 1452 a meal at Stirling Castle, which was intended as an act of reconciliation, ended in the King stabbing the eighth Earl. The Earl's brothers harboured a grudge and the ninth Earl had treasonable dealings with England, and in 1455 James II marched against him. The Earl's brothers were killed, he fled south, and Threave was besieged with the royal artillery. The castle had recently been altered, a detached hall having been demolished and a curtain wall with corner towers built around the tower. It fell, but subsequent payments to officers of the garrison suggest that bribery was more successful than the cannon.

Threave was later a royal castle, with the Maxwells keepers of it and the Stewartry of Kirkcudbright from 1526 onwards. It was captured from them by the Regent Arran in 1545, was briefly surrendered in 1588 to James VI and was finally destroyed after surrender on honourable terms to the Covenanters in 1640 following a siege of thirteen weeks.

Urr NX 815647
This large motte, standing entirely within a large bean-shaped bailey, was the chief castle of the Lord of Galloway.

WIGTOWN DISTRICT

Auchness NX 106447
The tiny square sixteenth-century tower is much altered.

Baldoon NX 426536
Just one ivy-mantled side remains of the Dunbars' mansion.

Balzieland NX 097428
A fragment of a sixteenth-century tower of the McDoualls is incorporated in the garden wall of Logan House.

Barholm NX 521529
On the side of Barholm Hill high above the sea is the McCullochs' well hidden ruined L-plan tower of about 1570-1600.

Carsluith NX 495542 (AM*)
The ruined early sixteenth-century tower of the Brouns lies in a farmyard by the A75 coast road. The stair wing is an addition dated 1564 with the initial B. The Catholic Brouns feuded with the Protestant M'Cullochs of Barholm, and in 1579 Broun of Carsluith was fined £40 after his son John failed to account for having murdered M'Culloch of Barholm.

Clanyard NX 109374
A fragment remains of a Gordon L-plan castle of about 1580-1600.

Corsewall NX 991715
At the north tip of the Rinns of Galloway is the basement of a fifteenth-century tower of the Stewarts of Dreghorn.

Craigcaffie NX 089641
The empty tower with parapets on the end gables only is dated 157?, with initials of John Neilson and Margaret Strang.

Craighlaw NX 305611
Within the mansion is the basement of a tower. A reset stone of the early sixteenth century has the arms of William Gordon and his Baillie wife, and another is dated 1644.

Cruggleton NX 484428

In the thirteenth century Elena of Galloway and her husband, the Earl of Winchester, built a thick wall around a small enclosure on the summit of a clifftop motte with a bailey on the landward side. Edward Bruce captured the castle from the Comyns in 1308 and destroyed it, but the Douglases later repaired it and added a tower in the late fourteenth century.

In the 1570s the Regent Moray was asked for help by Robert Stewart, Commendator of Whithorn Priory, who was being besieged in 'the hous of Crugiltoun' by John, fifth Lord Fleming. In 1579 the Privy Council ordered it to be given to Margaret Stewart, widow of Andro Stewart, to whom it was feued by the Commendator. However, in December Cruggleton was captured in a night attack by the Commendator and Stewart of Garlies. In 1613 James Kennedy of Cruggleton seized Alexander Myrtoun and imprisoned him in the castle, for which he was denounced as a rebel, though he was acquitted because a charge was wrongly addressed. He got into debt and in 1620 sold the castle to Andrew Agnew of Lochnaw, who pulled it down for the materials. The remains were excavated in the early 1980s.

Dunragit NX 150582 and 148568

The house incorporates part of an old tower. Nearby, in a clearing behind trees, is the fine motte of Droughdool.

Dunskey NX 004534

In 1496 William Adair's castle was captured and burnt by Sir Alexander M'Culloch of Myrton and Uchtred McDouall of Garthland in retribution for Adair's involvement in the murder of Dionysius of Hamilton in Wigtown. The attackers were ordered to pay compensation but were granted remission in 1503. The existing L-plan tower with an adjoining wing, occupying the neck of a coastal promontory, was built in the 1580s by a later William Adair. He tortured the abbot of nearby Saulseat Abbey at Dunskey in an attempt to make him sign away the abbey lands. The castle was sold to Hugh Montgomery in 1620 and from 1660 to 1666 was held by John Blair, minister of Portpatrick. By the 1680s it was a ruin.

Galdenoch NX 974633

By a farm is a small ruined L-plan tower dated 1547 with the initials of Gilbert Agnew, son of the laird of Lochnaw.

Garlies NX 422692

The overgrown remains of the castle of the Stewarts lie halfway up a slope far from any roads. They include the lower part of a tower of about 1470-1500, like that of Cardoness.

Isle of Whithorn NX 466366

In the middle of the tiny port is an L-plan tower of about 1600 standing on a knoll. An adjacent range has a stone with the date 1674 and the initials of Patrick Houston and Margaret Gordon. Alterations were made to the tower when it was the home of Sir John Reid, Superintendent of the Coastguard.

Kennedy NX 111609 (P)

Until after 1789 the site of this castle was an island. John, Lord Kennedy, was keeper of it for the Crown in 1482, but the present ruin was built about 1600-10 for the Kennedy fifth Earl of Cassillis. It has a lofty main block with two square towers at one end with turrets in the re-entrant angles. The castle passed to Sir John Dalrymple, later Earl of Stair, who added the low extension to the north. It was not restored after being accidentally burnt in 1716.

Killasser NX 098451

Only the base remains of a M'Culloch tower of about 1500.

Lochnaw NX 994633 and 991628

On an islet in the loch is a fragment of a tower which existed by 1363, when Andrew Agnew was made its constable. It was destroyed in 1390 by Archibald the Grim. In the early sixteenth century the Agnews replaced it by a small square tower on the shore at the other end of the loch. The inscription on it, *Dom Andreas Agnew 1426 Nomen Fortissima Turris,* is a bogus addition of much later date. The mansion adjoining has dormer windows dated 1633 with the initials of Andrew Agnew and Anna Stewart. A wing was added in 1704 and more extensions were made in the nineteenth century. Part of the building is now used as a restaurant.

Mochrum NX 308541 and 294541

In 1474 the barony of Mochrum was divided between the second and third daughters of Patrick Dunbar. The second daughter and her husband, Sir John Dunbar, then built a tower, which, along with an adjacent T-planned seventeenth-century building, was restored from ruin and incorporated in a mansion by the Marquis of Bute, who bought the property in 1878. The third daughter and her husband, Patrick Dunbar, walled in an island in nearby Castle Loch and converted a thirteenth-century chapel on it into a hall. This is now very ruinous.

Myrton NX 360432

The tower house, of which the surviving half has been converted into a dovecot, was probably erected by Sir Alexander

M'Culloch after 1504, when James IV visited his Master Falconer here and raised his lands into a barony. An unfortified house was added a few years before the property was sold to Sir William Maxwell in 1685. The ruins are hidden by trees and ivy within the Monreith estate.

Park NX 189571 (AM)
An inscription above the entrance of this L-plan tower records 'Blessit Be The Name Of The Lord. This Verk Vas Begvn The First Day Of March 1590 Be Thos Hay Of Park And Ionet Mak Dovel His Spovs.' The empty building has lost its outbuildings but was restored and reharled in the 1970s.

Port NX 426358
A headland near St Ninian's Cave has the last remains of a tiny court with a wall defending the two landward sides.

Sinniness NX 205531
Only a fragment remains of the substantial tower built about 1600 by Archibald Kennedy, and later held by the Stairs.

Sorbie NX 451471
The ruined L-plan tower of Alexander Hannay, who died about 1615, lies in a clearing in woods and is similar to Park Castle. A feud with the Murrays of Broughton, resulting in a series of disturbances involving the Stewarts of Garlies, the Dunbars and the Kennedys, impoverished the Hannays, and in 1626 much of their lands had to be sold to Sir Patrick Agnew of Lochnaw and Stewart of Garlies, while in 1640 John Hannay was killed in a quarrel. Stewart of Garlies, by then Earl of Galloway, got Sorbie in 1677, and the last inhabitant was Brigadier-General Stewart, who died in 1748.

Stranraer NX 061608
After years of neglect, the Adairs' sixteenth-century L-plan tower, later held by the Kennedys and the Stairs, has been restored. In the late seventeenth century the tower was heightened above the original open battlements and given a bell turret for use as the town jail. It was then the base of Graham of Claverhouse when oppressing the local Covenanters.

Wigg NX 431430
The tower bears the date 1593 and the initials and arms of Archibald Stewart of Bardye and Tonderghie and Helen M'Kerlie. A round stair tower and a stair turret at opposite corners were removed when the tower became the nucleus of a mansion, now ruined and disguised by trees, bushes and ivy.

41

Fife Region

Aberdour NT 193854 (AM)
The much damaged late thirteenth-century tower house is one of the earliest in Scotland. It passed to the Douglases in 1342. This branch of the family became Earls of Morton and in the sixteenth and seventeenth centuries added a courtyard and various apartments, some of which are still roofed.

Airdrie NO 567084
The mansion includes the stair wing of James Lumsdaine's castle dated 1586. Sold in 1602 to William Turnbull, it was later held by Sir John Preston and then General Anstruther.

Aithernie NO 379035
In a field is a fragment of the Riggs family's castle.

Ardross NO 509007
By the sea is the basement of the Dishingtons' fifteenth-century tower and a later range. The castle was sold to William Scot in 1607 and later acquired by Sir William Anstruther.

Balcarres NO 476044
John Lindsey's Z-plan castle of 1595 is part of a mansion.

Balcomie NO 626099
Mary of Guise was entertained here after landing in 1538 but the remains now incorporated in a farm are later. Towers stood at either end of a main block, of which about a third remains intact. A former barmkin on the north had a gateway dated 1602 with the initials of James Learmouth.

Balfour NO 324003
The core of the very ruinous house is a massively walled vaulted basement of the sixteenth century.

Balgonie NO 313007
About 1480-90 Robert Lundie, Lord High Treasurer, added a hall block and barmkin to the Sibbalds' tower of about 1450. The south wall of the court is a sixteenth-century rebuilding while the east range was built in two phases by General Alexander Leslie, created Earl of Leven in 1641.

Balmbreich NO 272205
Though later considerably altered and now ruined, this was a late fourteenth-century courtyard castle of the Leslies, later Earls of Rothes, created Dukes in 1680. The block on the south side originally contained a chapel over cellars.

Balmuto NT 221898
The mansion includes a modest fifteenth-century tower with sixteenth-century additions. It bears the dates 1594 and 1680 with initials respectively of John Boswell and Isabella Sandilands and David Boswell and Margaret Paterson.

Balwearie NO 252904
Only half remains of the tower which James III licensed William Scot to build in 1464.

Bandon NO 277043
The ruined late sixteenth-century tower of the Balfours of Balbirnie, with an added round turret, lies in a field.

Bordie NS 956869
At a farm is a wing of a seventeenth-century building.

Carden NT 227937
. The small ruined early sixteenth-century tower of the Martin family stands in the Raith estate.

Carslogie NO 353144
A fallen dormer pediment from the ruin has the date 1590 and the initials of George Clephane and Katherine Orme. A lintel reset in a nearby cartshed has the date 1710 and the initials of David Clephane and Joanna Colville.

Collairnie NO 307170
The surviving wing lies derelict adjoining a farm and bears the dates 1581 and 1607 with the initials of David Balfour and his wife, and of Hugh Balfour and his wife.

Corston NO 208098
The now much ruined late sixteenth-century tower of the Ramseys passed to the Colquhouns in 1669.

Couston NT 168851
A wing remains of the Logans' seventeenth-century mansion.

Craighall NO 407107
The Kinninmonds' mansion, with two wings on one side, joined by a later front dated 1691, and a third in the middle of the other side, was bought in 1635 by the lawyer Sir Thomas Hope and demolished in the mid twentieth century.

Creich NO 329212
The Bethunes' early sixteenth-century L-plan tower house on a crag has a square stair turret in the re-entrant angle.

Cruivie NO 419229
The massive ruined L-plan tower on a mound beside South Straiton Farm is probably the house which James Sandilands transferred to his namesake uncle in 1509. It was granted in 1540 to Henry Ramsey and later passed to the Carnegies.

Dairsie NO 414160
The Learmouths' now ruined Z-plan castle with two small round flanking towers was transferred to the Spottiswodes in 1616. Sir Robert Spottiswode, President of the Court of Session, was executed for his part in the Royalist rising of 1650. Dairsie then went to his father-in-law, George Morrison.

Denmylne NO 249175
The sixteenth-century castle of the Balfours has a wing in the middle of one side and a latrine turret on the other.

Earlshall NO 465211 (P)
Sir William Bruce's castle of 1546 onwards, restored in 1890, consists of a courtyard with the gateway on the east, a south range, an L-plan south-west tower, and the main house on the north, with a wing and stair at the south-west corner and a round tower on the north-east corner. The east side of the court is now open to the gardens.

Easter Kinnear NO 404232
A fragment of a late tower house stands west of the farm.

Falkland NO 254075 (AM)
Excavation has revealed the bases of two round towers of the thirteenth-century courtyard castle of the Earls of Fife. Here in 1402 David, Duke of Rothesay, heir of Robert III, was warded in the custody of his uncle the Duke of Albany after rebelling and died under dubious circumstances. After 1425 Falkland was retained by the Crown as a hunting seat. The east and south ranges and gatehouse are the work of James IV and James V. The latter was fond of Falkland and died there in 1542. Decay followed James VI's removal to London in 1603.

Fernie NO 316147
The Fernies' late sixteenth-century L-plan castle has a round tower on the outermost corner of the L. After passing to the Balfours in 1700, the main block was lengthened and given another round tower to balance the original one.

Fordell NT 147854
The restored Z-plan castle, with two square stair towers, of James Henderson and Jean Murray bears the date 1580 and has a reset stone from an older building burnt down in 1568.

Hallyards NT 212914

Only fragments and foundations remain of the Skenes' courtyard castle of the sixteenth and seventeenth centuries.

Isle of May NT 659991

In the mid sixteenth century Patrick Learmouth created a castle, now ruined, out of a building of a former Cluniac priory by adding a round tower with gunports to one corner.

Kellie NO 520052 (P)

The mansion of the fifth Lord Oliphant bears the date 1606 and is T-planned with three towers, the northern having originally been an early sixteenth century tower house, and the eastern being an L-plan tower dated 1573 with the initials of Margaret Hay, wife of Laurence, fourth Lord Oliphant. In 1613 the castle was bought by Sir Thomas Erskine of Gogar, who was high in the favour of James VI for assisting the King at the Gowrie conspiracy of 1600. He was created Earl of Kellie in 1619. After the death of the tenth Earl the castle became ruinous but was restored by James Lorimer, Professor of Public Law at Edinburgh University, in the 1870s.

Kilconquhar NO 494027

The L-plan late sixteenth-century tower of the Bellendens was sold to Sir John Carstairs in 1640 and is now the nucleus of the Earl of Crawford's nineteenth-century mansion.

Killernie NT 033924

The Scotts' ruined Z-plan castle has two small round turrets.

Kirkton NO 458258

The ruined mansion has one round corner tower. A lintel from it, with the date 1585 and the arms and initials of David Balfour and Catherine Crichton, is at Kirkton Barnes. The mansion later passed to the Youngs and another stone has the date 1645 and the initials of David Young and Elizabeth Nairn. In 1700 it was acquired by John Gillespie of Newton Rires.

Knockdavie NT 213883

The home of a Douglas opponent of the Covenanters is a late and much ruined mansion without defensive features.

Largo NO 418034

Sir Andrew Wood was licensed to build a castle in 1491 in reward for valuable military service to James IV, but the one small round conical-roofed tower that remains is about a century later. It was sold to Alexander Durham in 1662 and about a century later his descendants dismantled most of the castle and constructed a new house on the site.

Loch Ore NT 175959
The mound on which the shattered overgrown fragments lie may be a motte and was an island in a loch until about 1800. In the fourteenth century it passed from the Lochore family to the Valances, who then built a square tower and a thin surrounding barmkin wall. The Wardlows of Torrie added now destroyed round turrets to the barmkin wall. In the mid seventeenth century it passed to John Malcolm of Balbedie.

Lordscairnie NO 348178
Alexander Lindsay, fourth Earl of Crawford, built this ruined fifteenth-century tower, later used as a church.

Lundin NO 399029
Only an altered stair turret survived demolition in 1876.

Macduff's NT 344972
The late fourteenth-century courtyard castle of John de Wemyss was entered by a self-contained gate tower at one landward corner. It passed to the Livingstones and then in 1530 to the Colvilles of Ochiltree, who built a second tower, now the main surviving part, and a range linking the two, together with a new entrance below apartments. Later a new seaward wall was built, reducing the size of the court, and an outer court with gunports and corner turrets was built to landward. The castle decayed after going in 1630 to John Wemyss, later Earl of Wemyss, who had several other castles.

Malcolm Canmore's NT 087873
In Dunfermline Park is the defaced base of a massive tower on top of a rock rising high above the Tower Burn. It has no connection with the eleventh-century king and is much more likely to be of the fourteenth century.

Monimail NO 299141
The small square tower, bearing the date 1578 and the initials of Sir James Balfour of Pittendreich, formed one wing of an L-plan house replacing or adapted from a house of the Archbishops of St Andrews which was decayed in 1564.

Mountquhanie NO 347212
The ruined sixteenth-century tower was later given a courtyard with outbuildings and a round dovecot turret. It bears the date 1597 and the Balfour arms and initials on the still inhabited house. It passed to the Lumsdens and later to the Crawfords, a datestone of 1683 relating to the latter. The tower was supposedly habitable until about 1800.

Myres NO 242110
The castle has two adjoining square blocks with tiny round turrets on the diagonally opposite outer corners. Begun probably by the Scrymgeours, it passed in 1611 to the Patersons, and the initials of a Paterson and his wife, with the date 1619, appear on the top of one turret. The opposite end is now submerged within a nineteenth-century mansion.

Naughton NO 373246
On a rock by Naughton House are the remains of a tower and barmkin built by the Crichtons in the sixteenth century. The estate later returned to the original owners, the Hays, and a reset panel has the date 1625 and the initials of Peter and Marjory Hay. A drawing of 1760 shows the tower house on the east side with a round turret at the south-east corner and a range of outbuildings on the north side.

Newark NO 518012
The ruined sixteenth-century castle of the Sandilands of Cruivie has a modest rectangular courtyard with the sea on two sides, apartments on a third, and a wall and gate on the fourth, flanked by a round corner tower. A bankrupt Sir James Sandilands sold the castle in 1649 to the Covenanter General David Leslie, who made additions and alterations.

Otterston NT 165852
The much altered house with a court with two towers bears the date 1589 and the initials of D. Mowbray and his wife.

Parboath NO 322176
In a field is a fragment of a vaulted basement cellar.

Pitcairlie NO 236148
The seat of the Earls of Rothes, then the Leslies of Lindores and later the Cathcarts, is a much extended and altered Z-plan castle of the late sixteenth century.

Pitcruvie NO 413046
Lord Lindsay's ruined tower of about 1500 lies by a farm.

Pitcullo NO 413196
The late sixteenth-century L-plan castle of the Balfours, and later the Trents, has a round stair turret in line with a crosswall. A later wing balancing the original one was removed in a restoration from ruin in the 1970s and 1980s.

Pitfirrane NT 060863
The Halketts' fifteenth-century L-plan tower was raised by a storey and given turrets with the date 1583 and the arms and initials of George Halkett and Jean Hepburn. A south-east wing was added in the seventeenth century. The yett now forms a gate leading out into the gardens.

Pitreavie NT 117847
This mansion with gunports and two wings on the same side bears the initials of Sir Henry Wardlaw, chamberlain to James VI's consort Anne, and who died in 1638.

Pittarthie NO 522091
The ivy-mantled ruin dates from about 1598 when the lands were surrendered by James Monypennie and granted to Andrew Logan. The building is an L-plan with the wing flanking two sides of the main block. It was acquired by the Bruces in 1644.

Pitteadie NT 257891
The Vallances' now ruined late fifteenth-century tower later passed to the Sandilands. In 1612 the estate was made a barony for John Boswell and later passed to the Calderwoods.

Pittencrieff NT 087873
The T-plan house has the date 1610 and the initials of Sir Alexander Clerk. It was heightened by one storey in 1731.

Randerston NO 608108
The Myrtouns' late sixteenth-century L-plan castle with a wing flanking two sides of the main block is now a farmhouse. A predecessor existing in 1528 stood half a mile (800 m) to the east. Michael Balfour bought it in 1663, and Balfours still own it.

Ravenscraig NT 291925
This coastal promontory fortress, the first in Britain to be designed for defence against artillery, was begun about 1460 for Mary of Gueldres, widow of James II, and was left unfinished at her death in 1464. Facing the higher ground is a screen wall containing the entrance and cellars and which was intended to have a hall above. At either end is a large D-shaped tower, one of which was a tower house. The position is stronger than it looks for early guns could not fire downhill. In 1470 the castle was given to William Sinclair, Earl of Caithness, in partial exchange for the earldom of Orkney.

Rossend NT 225859
The nucleus of the house is an L-plan tower bearing the date 1554, and built by George Dury, the legitimised son of the

Commendator of Dunfermline Abbey. Later owners were the Melvilles and Wemysses, who made additions to the west side.

Rosyth NT 115820 (AM: written permission required)
This ruin stood on an island until the land was reclaimed for use as a naval dockyard. It has a massive fifteenth-century tower house with a stair wing and inserted mullion and transom windows dated 1635 and initialled EI and SMN. The fragmentary courtyard has a gateway dated 1561 with the initials of Queen Mary, commemorating her landing at Leith.

St Andrews NO 513169
The castle lies on the rocky shore close to the ruined cathedral and was founded by Bishop Roger about 1200 as a rectangular enclosure of earth and timber with a square stone gatehouse. It was dismantled by Robert Bruce's forces but in 1336 it and the now destroyed Leuchars Castle were rebuilt by the English in support of Edward Balliol. The gateway was then extended southwards. Sir Andrew Moray in 1337 captured the castle and 'to the erd dang it doun'.

Bishop Trail (1385-1401) rebuilt the castle, surrounding the court with a stone wall with two towers facing seawards. One tower contains a bottle dungeon hollowed out of the rock. The gateway became a tower house with a new entrance nearby.

Patrick Graham, the first Archbishop, was deposed and held prisoner within his own castle before confinement at Iona, Dunfermline and Loch Leven, where he died in 1478. Archbishop Alexander Stewart was killed at Flodden in 1513 and during subsequent squabbling over the see one contender, Gavin Douglas, occupied the castle but was driven out by Prior John Hepburn, who filled both castle and cathedral with 'men, weapons and artillery'. James Beaton, Archbishop from 1523 to 1539, was succeeded by his nephew, the celebrated Cardinal David Beaton. During the unrest following James V's death in 1542 the Cardinal strengthened the castle by adding two round blockhouses, now destroyed, to the landward corners. However, in 1546 a party of Protestants succeeded in gaining admission along with the masons and they murdered Beaton. Reinforced by others, including the fiery preacher John Knox, and provisioned by sea from England, they then held the castle for a year against the regency. The besiegers tunnelled towards the walls, and the defenders countermined and captured their tunnel. Both tunnels still survive. It was only when a French fleet cut off English aid that the garrison surrendered and became galley slaves. The castle was annexed to the Crown in 1587 and given to the Earl of Dunbar in 1606 but restored to the revived bishopric in 1612. The Castle had lost its importance and in 1654 the town council had the harbour repaired with stone from it.

Scotstarvit NO 370113 (AM)

This fine ashlar-faced L-plan tower house was built some time between 1550 and 1579. The top room, level with the parapet, formerly had an ornate fireplace with the date 1627 and the initials of Sir John Scot and Dame Anne Drummond. In it Sir John probably wrote his famous satirical book, *Scot of Scotstarvit's Staggering State of the Scots Statesmen.*

Seafield NT 280885

The Moultrays' tower went to the Earl of Melville after the last of them was killed in the 1715 Jacobite rebellion. The ruined fifteenth-century tower, with a stair turret projecting from one end wall, stands on a rock by the shore and has remains of a former surrounding barmkin wall.

Strathendry NO 226020

The late sixteenth-century T-plan castle of the Forresters of Carden passed to the Douglases and was later modernised. It has the date 1699 and the initials of Sir Edward Douglas.

Struthers NO 377097

Only fragments remain of a late sixteenth-century L-planned house, court and outbuildings of Lord Lindsey of Byres.

Tulliallan NS 927888

The thirteenth-century hall house of the Blackadders has some unusual details and internal arrangements. It has three entrances at ground level and fine ribbed vaults.

Wemyss NT 329951

A fifteenth-century tower and barmkin by the shore were given apartments and a round flanking tower either by Sir David Wemyss, who was killed at Flodden in 1513, or by his son. The buildings were heightened in the seventeenth century and a long L-shaped wing bearing the dates 1652 and 1671 was added to the south. The Earls of Wemyss have made many later alterations and some additions to the west.

Grampian Region

BANFF AND BUCHAN DISTRICT

Banff NJ 689643

About a third of the walling of the Comyns' thirteenth-century castle of enclosure remains behind the house of 1750 built by James Ogilvie, sixth Earl of Findlater.

Boddam NK 124419
Except for the gateway, only foundations remain of a sixteenth-century courtyard castle with apartments on all sides, built by the Keiths of Ludquharn on a headland.

Boyne NJ 612657
Above the Boyne Burn is a very shattered and overgrown courtyard castle with four round corner towers and a twin-turreted gatehouse built by Sir George Ogilvie of Dunlugas after 1575 to replace an older castle nearer the sea.

Byth NJ 614565
Only a fragment and some heraldry remain of the castle built by the Forbes family in 1593.

Cairnbulg NK 016640
In the 1550s Sir Alexander Fraser created a Z-plan castle by adding a long main block with one round tower to a tower house of about 1380-1400 and later. After a new family seat of 1666 and later at Philorth nearby was burnt down in 1915 the Fraser Lord Saltoun moved back to Cairnbulg, which had been restored in 1896-7 for John Duchie, a shipowner.

Carnousie NJ 670504
The Ogilvies' sixteenth-century Z-plan castle with a square wing and a round tower has now been restored after use as a piggery. In 1622 George Ogilvie complained to the Privy Council about Robert Innes's depredations on the estate.

Clackriack NJ 933471
Just one corner remains of a late tower of the Keiths.

Delgatie NJ 755506
The much altered and massive L-plan tower of George Hay, seventh Earl of Errol, contains a rib-vaulted laird's room in the wing dated 1570, with the comment 'My Hoyp Is In Ye Lord'. Part of the west wall was battered down by James VI's forces during a six-week siege in 1594. Sir William Hay was executed in Edinburgh after being Montrose's chief of staff during the campaign of 1650. Delgatie was later held by the Duffs and the Ainslies but is now a Hay possession again.

Dundarg NJ 895649
The Comyns' thirteenth-century castle, with a narrow inner court on a promontory and a D-shaped outer court with a rectangular keep, was destroyed by the Bruces in 1308 but was rebuilt by Henry de Beaumont in 1334. In that year it was besieged, captured and destroyed again by the Regent Moray.

The site was briefly refortified about 1550 by Lord Borthwick and a house of 1938 now stands in the outer part of the ruin.

Eden NJ 698588
The Meldrums' L-plan castle bears the date 1577 on a lintel. George Leslie extended it in the 1670s and in 1712 the castle was sold to William Duff. It is now a ruin.

Fedderate NJ 897498
In a field are two lofty fragments of a Gordon L-plan tower of about 1570, captured by William III's forces in 1689.

Findlater NJ 542673
Sir Walter Ogilvie was licensed to fortify this coastal promontory in 1445. A ruinous palace block lies on one side of a long court of irregular shape. The Ogilvies became Earls of Findlater in 1638, though Cullen was then their main seat.

Fordyce NJ 556638
In the village is a small L-plan tower with ornamental shotholes, built in 1592 by Thomas Menzies of Aberdeen.

Forglen NJ 696517
The Abercrombies' mansion of 1842 incorporates old parts and has a reset stone with the date 1577.

Fyvie NJ 764393
There was an early royal castle here but the existing building originated as a courtyard castle with square corner towers built for Sir James Lindsay about 1390-1400. One tower is named after the next owner, Sir Henry Preston, and another after the Meldrums, owners from 1440 to 1596. It then went to Alexander Seton, Lord Fyvie and Earl of Dunfermline. He built the west wing with its remarkable stair and added the ornamental top features to the south range. Fyvie was then still a courtyard castle although two wings have now entirely gone. General Gordon, son of the second Earl of Aberdeen, added the Gordon Tower about 1750. The castle is now L-planned and owned by Forbes-Leith baronets.

Hatton NJ 758469
The Duffs' mansion of 1820 incorporates four round towers of the sixteenth-century castle of Balquhollie. It was the seat of the Monte Altos or Mowats until sold in 1723.

Inchdrewer NJ 656607
This L-plan tower and courtyard with one round flanking tower were built by the Ogilvies of Boyne about 1600 to provide

a seat for the eldest son. The Ogilvie Lord Banff in 1642 added a wing to the tower. In 1713 Lord Banff was murdered here and the castle burnt out. It was restored in the 1960s.

Inverallochy NK 041629
The ruined sixteenth-century castle of the Commings has a small quadrangular court with a gabled tower house in one corner and two ranges of apartments facing each other.

Inverugie NK 102484
The Keith Earl Marischal's ruined castle of about 1580-1600 was blown up in 1899. The main block had two round towers facing the field and a stair turret facing a court towards the river. Over the courtyard gateway was the date 1670 with the initials of Earl William and Anna Douglas. The basement remains.

Kineddar NJ 722562
By a bend of the A947 are the ruins of a Comyn thirteenth-century courtyard castle destroyed by the Bruces about 1308.

Kinnaird's Head NK 999677
The tower house on the north side of Fraserburgh was built by Sir Alexander Fraser of Philorth at about the time he founded the port in 1569. In the nineteenth century a lighthouse was built upon it. On the shore close by is the Wine Tower of about the same date. It has three vaulted storeys.

Kinnairdy NJ 609498
Sir Alexander Innes and Dame Christian Dunbar's lofty tower of about 1480-1500 has been altered at the top and given a wing. It was sold to Crichton of Frendraught, and in 1647 to the Reverend John Gregory, whose brother David made the first ever barometer there. Later the Inneses bought it back.

Park NJ 587571
A late sixteenth-century Z-plan Gordon castle is incorporated into a Duff mansion of 1829.

Pitgair NJ 764587
Only the barest traces of a tower survive.

Pitsligo NJ 928669
Sir William Forbes's massive tower house of about 1424-40 lies on the south side of a courtyard with a round tower and ranges on the three other sides. A stair turret bears the royal arms and the dates 1577 and 1603. The outer court gateway has the initials of Alexander Forbes, created Lord Pitsligo in 1633, and his wife, while over the inner gateway is the date 1663 with the initials of

Alexander, second Lord Pitsligo, and Lady Mary Erskine. The fourth Lord became a fugitive after the 1715 Jacobite rebellion but the castle was ruinous before then, the third storey of the tower house having been taken down in the early 1700s.

Pittullie NJ 945671

Though it bears the date 1651 on a skewstone, this long low ruined house with a high wing was probably built about 1596 for Alexander Fraser and Margaret Abernethy. It passed to the Cumines, who made additions and lived there till about 1850.

Ravenscraig NK 095488

In one corner of a triangular moated enclosure among trees above the Ugie is the Keiths' ruined L-plan tower licensed in 1491 and second in size only to Borthwick.

Slains NK 102362

In the vast ruined mansion of 1836, inhabited by the Hay Earls of Errol until 1916, are two cellars of a castle developed out of the Tower of Bowness in 1597 by the ninth Earl to replace the destroyed castle of Old Slains.

GORDON AND ABERDEEN CITY DISTRICTS

Aberdeen NJ 944063

Nothing remains of Alexander III's stone castle, destroyed by the townsfolk after they stormed it in the Bruce interest in 1308. Two lofty blocks of flats stand on the site.

Arnage NJ 936370

The Cheynes' late sixteenth-century Z-plan castle with two square wings was sold in 1702 to James Ross, Provost of Aberdeen, and was restored in the 1930s by Donald Stewart.

Asloun NJ 542149

Only one round tower and a length of walling remain of John Cowdell's Z-plan castle of the 1560s. Here Montrose spent the night before defeating the Covenanters under General Baillie at the battle of Alford in 1645.

Aswanley NJ 445397

The Calders' altered L-plan house of about 1620 passed to the Duffs in 1768 and is now a farmhouse. It has a round stair turret on the north and to the south a courtyard dated 1692 over the gateway, with the initials of a Calder and a Skene.

Auchanachie NJ 498469

The small tower of the eldest son of Gordon of Avochie bears the date 1594 and the words 'From Ovr Enemies Defend Vs Ochrist'. There is a low seventeenth-century added wing.

Auchlossan NJ 571021
The Rosses' seventeenth-century house with shotholes around the entrance has been lowered, altered and added to.

Auchry NJ 788507
The only relic of the castle is a dormer pediment on the gable of the farmhouse with the initials of Patrick Cumming.

Avochie NJ 536466
This seventeenth-century Gordon house is much ruined.

Balbithan NJ 812189
The Chalmers' castle of about 1600 bears the date 1679 on a bartizan. This may be the date of the added wing.

Balfluig NJ 593153
East of Alford is the lofty, late sixteenth-century L-plan tower of the Forbeses of Corsindae. The estate became the barony of Alford in 1650 and was sold to the Farquharsons of Haughton in 1753. The castle was restored in the 1960s.

Balquhain NJ 732236
Balquhain was the chief seat of the Aberdeenshire Leslies from 1340 until burnt by Cumberland in 1746, and Queen Mary was entertained there in 1562. It consists of a ruinous tower house of the 1530s by a ravine, with on the other side the foundations of a court with various ranges.

Barra NJ 792258
The Setons' castle with a long main block and two round turrets, one adjoining a small wing, bears the dates 1614 and 1618. In 1615 Elizabeth Seton pursued at law James King, 'sumetyme of Barra', for killing her father at the castle. The wing was given a square extension with a third round turret about 1620-40 and the Ramseys added a wing about 1755.

Beldorney NJ 424369
George Gordon and Janet Rose's Z-plan castle of the 1550s has a round tower and a square stair turret. A courtyard to the west has over the entrance the initials of John and Anne Gordon with the date 1679. The castle was sold to the Grants in 1807 and was restored in the 1960s.

Bognie NJ 595450
The late ruined Morrison castle stands in a field.

Brux NJ 500169

The farmhouse and mill contain reset material from the Forbeses' castle, first mentioned in 1546.

Castle Fraser NJ 723126 (NT)

Thomas Fraser's tower house of about 1454-60, called Muchalls-in-Mar, was made into a Z-plan castle by Michael Fraser between 1565 and 1588 with the addition of a square tower and a round one. His son Andrew, created Lord Fraser in 1633, lengthened the main block and added the magnificent upper works with dormers, bartizans and a balustraded top to the round tower, and also the two courtyard ranges on the north. The main building has the date 1617 with the name of the master mason I. Bel, while the courtyard ranges bear the date 1631 and the initials of Lord Fraser, his wives and daughter-in-law. It was about this time that the name was changed to Castle Fraser. The grounds were ravaged by the Royalists in 1638 and 1645 but the castle survived unharmed, while Lord Fraser took refuge at Cairnbulg. The fourth Lord died a fugitive after the 1715 rebellion and the castle passed through various branches of the family before it was restored for the Pearsons in the 1920s and 1960s and then handed to the National Trust.

Castle Newe NJ 380124

Little remains of the Forbeses' T-plan castle of 1604, or of the large granite mansion that engulfed it in 1831.

Cluny NJ 688128

John Bell's masterpiece of the 1600s, built for Thomas Gordon on a Z-plan with two round towers, was shorn of all its attractive details and encased in a mansion of 1836-40.

Colquhonnie NJ 365126

By the Newe Arms Hotel is the lower part of a sixteenth-century L-plan tower house of the Forbeses of Towie.

Corgarff NJ 255086 (AM)

The Elphinstones' tower of about 1530 was later leased to the Forbeses. In 1571 Margaret Campbell, the wife of Forbes of Towie, and her household of twenty-six people were all burnt to death when the Gordons set the tower on fire. The castle was recovered by the Elphinstones and they complained to the Privy Council in 1607 that Alexander Forbes had taken the 'fortalice of Torgarffa' by breaking in the door with 'grete geistis, foir hammeris' etc, and subsequently held it as a 'house of war' with the assistance of 'Highland Thieves and limmers'. As part of the Mar earldom, the tower went to the Erskines in 1626. It was used as a mustering point by Montrose in his campaign of 1645 and in

1689 was burnt to deny the use of it to the government forces. After further use as a mustering point in the 1715 rebellion led by the Earl of Mar, it was forfeited and passed to the Forbeses. They in turn were forfeited after the 1745 rebellion, in which the tower was used again by Jacobite troops. In 1748 the Hanoverian government took it over, greatly altered the tower, added a pair of single-storey barrack wings and surrounded it by a star-shaped chemise with musketry loops in the wall. A Highland peace-keeping garrison was then stationed there for many years.

Corsindae NJ 686088

Incorporated in the whitewashed mansion is the tower of John Forbes, who was arrested in 1605 as one of 'the insolent society of boys denounced for slaughter and other enormities' and had to be closely guarded all the way to Edinburgh for fear of rescue attempts by his kinsmen.

Craig NJ 472248

Above the Den of Craig is a large L-plan tower built for William Gordon in the 1570s and held by his descendants until 1892. It replaced a motte by the church and bears the royal arms and those of William's grandfather, Patrick, and his father, William, with those of their wives. The tower is the most complete and unaltered of a series including Gight, Delgatie and Towie Barclay, all built for Catholic lairds. Each has a rib-vaulted entrance lobby connected to a stair in a far outer wall of the L by a passage, while the wing contains the laird's room set over the warmth of the kitchen. The tower is adjoined by a tiny courtyard of 1726.

Craigievar NJ 566095 (NT)

This famous castle was begun at the end of the sixteenth century by the Mortimers. They fell into debt and in 1610 sold the unfinished L-plan tower to the wealthy merchant William Forbes. He employed the Bells to finish the castle and with the bold mouldings, bartizans, dormers, ogival domes and a balustrade on the outside and with magnificent plasterwork and panelling inside they created a masterpiece. On the panelling appear the arms and initials of Master William Forbes and his wife, Margery Woodward. The tower stood in one corner of a square barmkin, of which only the leaning west wall and south-west corner turret survive. The second William Forbes was made a baronet in 1630 and in 1884 the eighth baronet became the seventeenth Lord Sempill.

Craigston NJ 762550

The lofty house which the Bells built for John Urquhart has two gabled wings on the same side. On it is inscribed 'This Vark

Foundit Ye Fourtene Of March Ane Thousand Sex Hounder Four Yeiris And Endit Ye 8 Of December, 1607'.

Davidston NJ 429451

The date 1678 and the inscription 'IG and TA builded this house' on a bartizan may refer to the addition of a wing to a sixteenth-century Gordon tower. The house and its courtyard were restored from dereliction in the 1970s.

Drum NJ 796005 (NT)

The massive tower house which Richard Cementarius (mason) was building for Alexander III at the time of the king's death in 1286 is the only one of its period to remain complete with the original plain battlements carried on a single row of corbels. In 1323 Robert Bruce granted it to his armourbearer and secretary, Sir William Irvine. His grandson Alexander and Maclean of Duart killed each other at the battle of Harlaw, fought near Balquhain in 1411. The ninth Irvine laird, the seventh successive Alexander, added a court and a substantial mansion with two square towers. It bears the date 1619 with the initials of him and his wife. The castle was plundered by Argyll in 1644 and was altered and extended in the nineteenth century.

Druminnor NJ 513264

Druminnor, or Castle Forbes, has a palace block with a round stair turret and a rectangular tower at the ends of the side facing the former courtyard. James, second Lord Forbes, was licensed to build this in 1457 but work probably began on it as early as 1440. In 1571 it was sacked by the Gordons and the Master of Forbes taken off to Spynie Palace. About 1660 three armorial panels were set up on the stair turret commemorating the then Master of Forbes, his wife, Jean Campbell, and William, seventh Lord Forbes, and his wife, Elizabeth Keith, with the date 1577. The castle was sold in 1770, became neglected and was restored in the 1960s by the Hon Margaret Forbes-Sempill. The rectangular tower was taken down about 1800 by the Grants.

Dunnideer NJ 613282

On a hill near Insch is Sir Jocelyn de Balliol's ruined tower of 1260, supposedly occupied by the Tyries until 1724.

Ellon NJ 960307

North-east of the town is a ruined castle of the Kennedys, outlawed for a murder in 1652 and forced to sell up. The castle was extended by the Gordons but in 1782 most of it was cleared away and a new mansion built. This in turn was removed in the 1920s when its stable block was altered into a new mansion, with the ruin left lying by its approach.

Esslemont NJ 932298

A castle here was destroyed in 1493 during the course of a feud between the Cheynes and the Hays of Ardendracht. The base of an L-plan tower, which Henry Cheyne was licensed to build in 1500, was discovered in 1938. About 1580-1600 this tower was in turn replaced by the present ruined L-plan building, which incorporates on the outermost angle a round tower surviving from a courtyard with at least two more such towers. In 1646 Captain Blackwater led part of the Fyvie garrison to Esslemont to drive out a force of Covenanters, thirty-six of whom were killed, horses and arms being seized. The Earl of Errol sold Esslemont to the Gordons in 1728.

Fetternear NJ 723171

The present ruin comprises a tower built by William Leslie in the 1560s, considerable extensions of the 1690s built by Patrick Leslie, a Catholic who had become a Count of the Holy Roman Empire, and later additions. In front of it are traces of an early L-plan tower of the Bishops of Aberdeen.

Fichlie NJ 459149

The large mound bears traces of a thin enclosure wall.

Frendraught NJ 620418

Beside the house is a fragment of a Crichton castle burnt in 1630 during a feud with the Gordons. Six Gordons, including the laird of Rothiemay and Lord Aboyne, then died within it, the laird of Frendraught being tried but acquitted of their murder. His son was made Viscount Frendraught in 1642 and, although a Covenanter, fought for Montrose in 1650.

Gight NJ 827392

On a shelf by the den of the Ythan are a substantial ruined L-plan tower built in the 1570s for William Gordon and some outbuildings of late date. Many of the male members of this branch of the Gordons died violently and William Gordon was among those murdered. Catherine Gordon took Gight to the Hon John Byron, who sold it in 1787 to the Earl of Aberdeen to pay off debts. Their son was Lord Byron.

Glenbuchat NJ 387149 (AM*)

The ruin is a fine example of a Z-plan fortified house with two square towers, furnished with round bartizans and shotholes, set at opposite corners of a three-storey main block. On the tower containing the entrance is a square bartizan which contained a bell. Over the doorway is the illegible inscription 'Iohrn Gordon Helen Carnege 1590 Nothing on Earth Remanis Bot Faime'. John Gordon of Badenyon was accused of complicity in the murder of the Earl of Moray at Donibristle in 1592 and during the Catholic rebellion of 1594 Glenbuchat was occupied by James VI's forces. Later John's sons quarrelled with each other and their mother over possession of the castle. It passed to another branch of the family in 1701 and became the home of the celebrated Jacobite John Gordon, known as Old Glenbucket, who survived two rebellions to die in exile in Boulogne in 1750. The castle was sold in 1738 to Lord Braco and, by then a ruin, was sold again in 1883 and 1901.

Glenkindie NJ 437140
The large mansion of the Leiths incorporates a house built by the Strachan family in 1595.

Hallforest NJ 777154
This ruined fourteenth-century tower remained a secondary residence of the Keith Earls Marischal until the 1640s.

Harthill NJ 687252
The Leiths' interesting Z-plan castle dated 1601, with one round tower and one square one, was restored from ruin in the 1970s. A rare survival is the noble little barmkin gatehouse. Patrick Leith was executed by the Covenanters in 1647 while his brother quarrelled with the Provost of Aberdeen, was jailed and set his prison on fire.

Huntly NJ 532407 (AM)
The motte and bailey castle of Strathbogie was erected by Duncan, Earl of Fife. There Bruce lay recovering from an illness which struck him down during his campaign of 1307-8 against the Comyns. He later granted it to Sir Adam Gordon of Huntly in Berwickshire, Borders, but it was not until 1376 that the Gordons took full control of the lordship and built a massive L-plan tower house in the bailey. This and timber outbuildings were burnt by the Douglas Earl of Moray in 1452. Alexander Gordon, who had been created Earl of Huntly about 1446, afterwards began a massive new building called The Palace with a large round tower at one corner.

In 1496 Perkin Warbeck, a pretender to the English throne, was married here to Lady Catherine Gordon in the presence of James IV, and in 1506 the name was officially changed from Strathbogie to Huntly. George, fourth Earl, after travelling in France, had The Palace rebuilt above the basement to a more grandiose design. It bears the date 1553 and his initials and those of Elizabeth Keith. Although he was a Catholic like Queen Mary, she found him to be an overmighty subject (Huntly was nicknamed Cock o' the North) and in 1562 he was defeated in a battle at Corrichie. He died on the battlefield and his son John, a would-be suitor to Mary, was executed at Aberdeen. The castle was wrecked and had only just been restored by 1594, when the Gordons were defeated by James VI and a corner was blown out of The Palace. The Earl later made his peace with James and in 1599 he was created Marquis of Huntly, a rank recorded in an inscription put around the top of The Palace when it was restored and given a new stair turret in 1602.

The castle was captured by General Leslie in 1647 and the Royalist second Marquis was briefly a prisoner within it before execution at Edinburgh. Afterwards it fell into decay.

Invernochty NJ 352129

By the junction of the Nochty and the Don is the largest castle mound in Scotland, built for the Earl of Mar in the twelfth century. It has traces of a thick wall around the summit and formerly had a wet moat around the base.

Inverurie NJ 782206

The fine motte and bailey castle erected in the 1170s for David, Earl of the Garioch and Earl of Huntingdon, lies in a graveyard. It was used by the Bruce brothers in 1307-8.

Keith Hall NJ 787212

The Johnstons' late sixteenth-century Z-plan castle of Caskieben, with round turrets in the re-entrant angles, was bought in 1662 by Sir John Keith, third son of the sixth Earl Marischal. He was created Earl of Kintore for his part in saving the Crown Jewels from Cromwell at Dunnottar and he renamed Caskieben as Keith Hall. In the 1690s he added a new mansion on the south side with a symmetrical facade. The moat which surrounded a thirteenth-century timber house of the de Garioch family lies near the stableyard.

Kemnay NJ 733154

Sir Thomas Crombie's lofty L-plan tower of about 1600 was sold to the Burnetts in 1688 and each arm was later extended.

Kildrummy NJ 454164 (AM)

Alexander II began this large pentagonal courtyard castle in 1228 to dominate Mar and Moray and the route between them. The round keep or donjon called the Snow Tower, now ruined to its base, the round Warden's Tower, the hall between them and the two D-shaped towers were added under Alexander III about 1260-80, while Edward I is thought to have added the gateway, similar in plan to that at Harlech, about 1296-1303. The chapel of about 1250 curiously projects through the curtain wall with three vulnerable eastern lancet windows. As finished in about 1303, this is the most developed Scottish castle of its type.

Bruce had custody of Kildrummy in 1304 and sent here his queen and her ladies after his defeat at Methven in 1306. The castle was captured and dismantled by Prince Edward of Caernarfon through the treachery of Osborne the blacksmith, who set fire to it. Sir Nigel Bruce and his garrison were hanged while the ladies, who had escaped, were captured at Tain and sent south to England, where they were treated very badly. The castle was restored and in 1335 defended by Dame Christian Bruce against the Earl of Atholl, until the latter was drawn off, defeated and killed in the battle of Culblean by Dame Christian's husband, Sir Andrew de Moray.

The Earl of Mar was often host to David II here but in 1363, after a quarrel, the king besieged and captured the castle. In 1404 Isabella Douglas, Countess of Mar, was here seized by and forced to marry Sir Alexander Stewart, later the victor of Harlaw. After his death in 1435 the castle was retained by the Crown in spite of the claims of the Erskines. As Earls of Mar they finally obtained Kildrummy only in 1626 after it had been held by the Elphinstones for over a century. Sir Robert Erskine in desperation stormed the castle in 1442 but was forced to give it up, while in 1530 it was stormed by the freebooter John Strachan of Lynturk. Finally, in 1654 it was captured by Cromwellian forces. The Jacobites burnt Kildrummy in 1690 to deny use of it to the government but the Earl of Mar used it as his headquarters for the 1715 rebellion, which he led, after which it was dismantled.

Knockespoch NJ 544241

The nucleus of this Gordon house of various periods is a sixteenth-century tower visible on the south side.

Knockhall NJ 992265

This L-plan ruin, with a square stair turret on one of the long outer sides, was built by the third Lord Sinclair of Newburgh and bears the date 1565. It was sold in 1633 to the Udnys and was captured and plundered in 1639 by the Earl Marischal. The castle has been ruined since a fire in 1734, when the Udnys were saved by their fool, Jamie Fleeman.

Leith Hall NJ 541298 (NT)

The barmkin of James Leith's house of the 1650s with bartizans and dormers now contains later ranges on all sides.

Leslie NJ 599248

Although built as late as 1661 William Forbes's ruined L-plan castle still has vaulted cellars, bartizans and gunports. It was later sold to the Leiths and in the 1980s is being restored. The surrounding moat is probably a survival from an earlier timber manor house of the Leslies.

Lesmoir NJ 470280
About 1540 James Gordon built a stone castle on a motte and bailey site inhabited by Jock o' Scurdargue in the early fifteenth century. The castle was rebuilt in the 1590s by Alexander Gordon, whose son James was in 1625 created a baronet of Nova Scotia. In 1647 General Leslie captured the castle after a siege of two days by draining the wet moat. It was sold in 1759 to John Grant of Rothiemaise, who dismantled it. Only the scantiest traces survive.

Lickleyhead NJ 627237
William Leith's late sixteenth-century tower was given a stair wing and bartizans by John Forbes, who bought it in 1625. Patrick Duff added an east wing in the 1730s or 1740s, and an addition to this wing was made in the 1820s.

Lynturk NJ 598122
Only the barest traces survive of the sixteenth-century castle of the Strachans. Part of the moat is visible.

Midmar NJ 704053 and 701059
The Gordons' late sixteenth-century Z-plan castle has a square main block, with a square stair wing with bartizans, and a round tower with a parapet and an ogival domed stair turret. Later wings have been added to the two northern corners. The castle passed to the Forbeses, Grants, Davidsons, Elphinstones, Mansfields and Gordons again before being sold and restored in the 1960s. To the north-west, by the ruined church, is a twelfth-century castle mound.

Monymusk NJ 688155
The core of the house is William Forbes's L-plan tower of 1587 with a pair of shallow wings at adjacent corners. One round tower survives of the barmkin wall. The remainder of the building, including the two top storeys of the tower, was built by the Grants, who bought the property in 1712.

Mounie NJ 766287
John Seton's long low house of about 1580-1600 was given a stair turret with a square caphouse in the middle of one side after being bought in 1637 by Sir Robert Farquhar.

Old Slains NK 052301
The Hay Earls of Errol had a major stronghold on this coastal promontory until James VI had it blown up after the rebellion of 1594, and a new seat was developed later at new Slains. A lofty fragment of a tower of about 1370-1450 remains near a house built in 1950 by Diana, twenty-third Countess of Errol and High Constable of Scotland.

Pitcaple NJ 726261

The Z-plan castle of the Leslies of Balquhain has two round towers and considerable later extensions of the 1820s, when it was restored from ruin for the Lumsdens. Queen Mary was here in 1562, and Montrose, as a prisoner, in 1650.

Pitfichie NJ 677168

The castle has a rectangular block with a round tower at one corner and was restored from ruin in the 1980s. It was probably built by the Urrie family and was sold in 1597 to John Cheyne, who had David Bell working on it in 1607. It passed to the Monymusk Forbeses and was roofless by 1796.

Pitlurg NJ 436455

On a rock is one round flanking tower of a sixteenth-century courtyard castle of the Gordons.

Pittodrie NJ 697241

The core of the house, now a hotel, is an L-plan Erskine tower of 1605. A vaulted northern outbuilding has gunports.

Schivas NJ 898368

The L-plan house was built in the 1570s by Thomas Leiper for the Greys. Wings were added about 1750 and 1830 and after a fire in 1900 the house was rebuilt in the 'Balmoral baronial' style, only to have its original appearance restored in the 1930s for Lord Catto. The Greys were Catholic and an oratory in the hall has the letters IHS for Jesus, surmounted by a cross.

Skene NJ 768097

The nucleus of the Hamiltons' mansion is a fourteenth-century tower of the Skenes, now very much altered.

Strichen NJ 944549

In the garden of the Anderson and Woodman Library, in the village, well away from the site of the castle, is a dormer pediment with the year 1580 and Thomas Fraser's initials.

Terpersie NJ 547202

By a farm is William Gordon's shattered Z-plan castle with two round towers. It was formerly dated 1561 and remained intact until about 1900. Nothing remains of a kitchen wing added in the seventeenth century. The castle was burnt by General Baillie in 1645 and the last Gordon laird of the original line was executed after the 1745 rebellion.

Tillycairn NJ 664114

The L-plan tower, with a round stair turret in the re-entrant angle, bears stones with the initials of Matthew Lumsden, for whom it was built, and David Lumsden, who had it restored, with those of their wives and the dates 1550 and 1980. The building was a ruin from about 1700 to the 1970s.

Tillyfour NJ 659195

The Leslies' L-plan house of the sixteenth century bears the date 1626, referring to the time of Sir John Leslie, created a baronet in 1628. The house was restored about 1880.

Tillyhilt NJ 854318

Foundations remain of the castle of the Gordons.

Tolquhon NJ 873286 (AM)

Above the twin-turreted entrance to the main courtyard, which has apartments on all sides and flanking towers, square and round, at diagonally opposite corners, is the inscription 'Al This Warke Excep The Avld Tovr Was Begvn Be William Forbes 15 April 1584 And Endit Be Him 20 October 1589'. The 'Avld Tovr' was the tower house built by Sir John Forbes after his marriage to a Preston heiress in 1420. Alexander Forbes was knighted for saving Charles II's life at Worcester in 1651 but the family subsequently became impoverished and the estate was sold in 1716, though the last Forbes laird was not ejected until 1719. It went to the Earls of Aberdeen, who allowed it to fall into ruin.

Towie NJ 440129

The last remains of the Forbeses' L-plan castle of about 1620 were cleared away about 1970. Only the wing had survived.

Towie Barclay NJ 744439

This L-plan tower was built for Patrick Barclay between 1587 and 1593, the latter date appearing on it along with the year 1136, referring to when the Barclays first came here and raised an earth and timber castle. In 1639 the first shot of the Civil Wars was fired from the battlements when Walter Barclay and his wife's kinsmen, the Forbeses, defended themselves against a group of Royalist barons. In 1792 everything above the level of the remarkable ribbed vault over the hall was taken down and the castle was much decayed before being restored as a home in the 1970s.

Udny NJ 882268

The Udnys' tower of the late sixteenth and early seventeenth centuries with four round bartizans, was restored and later additions were removed in the 1960s for Margaret Udny Hamilton.

Warthill NJ 710315
On the mansion of 1845 are heraldic panels from the castle of the Leslies with the date 1686.

Waterton NJ 972305
A panel on the ruin gives the dates 1630 and 1770, referring to the period of tenure of the Forbes family.

Westhall NJ 673266
The Gordons' late sixteenth-century castle with one round tower and one square one on adjacent corners was sold in 1681 to James Horn, Vicar of Elgin. It later passed to the Dalrymple Elphinstones, who added the modern mansion.

KINCARDINE AND DEESIDE DISTRICT

Abergairn NO 358974
The Farquharsons' tiny tower of about 1600, with a round stair turret at a corner, is now destroyed down to the basement.

Abergeldie NO 287953
Alexander Gordon's tower house of about 1550, with a round tower with a square top, was in 1592 attacked by the Mackenzies in a raid known as the Great Spulzie. Dundee used it in 1689 as a mustering place for Jacobite rebels. It was captured by General Mackay and nearly fell to the Farquharsons, who were blockading it, in 1690. More recently the castle was used by guests and relatives of Queen Victoria at nearby Balmoral, including the Prince of Wales, before reverting to the Gordons. There are various later extensions.

Aboyne NO 526995
The Bissets had a motte here, afterwards used by Alexander III, but the present castle, which was restored and shorn of later extensions in the 1970s, is a much later building. It bears the date 1671 and the initials of Charles Gordon, first Earl of Aboyne, and Elizabeth Lyon, and it has two square wings.

Allardyce NO 818739
The late sixteenth-century L-plan tower of the Allardyce family, and later the Barclays, stands on a promontory and has through its base the entrance to a courtyard behind.

Arbuthnott NO 795750
Incorporating some remains of a stone building of 1242, Hugh Arbuthnott and Robert Arbuthnott in the fifteenth century created a courtyard with a gateway to the west, a hall block on the south and lesser apartments on the north. Further apart-

ments on the east were added in the sixteenth century, and some splendid ceilings were inserted about 1685. In 1755-7 the gateway was replaced by new parts, creating a mansion with a symmetrical west front, and the remaining old parts do not look castle-like. The Arbuthnotts became viscounts in 1644 and still live at the castle.

Auchenhove NJ 555024
Only scanty remains survive of the Duguids' castle burnt by Cumberland's forces in 1746.

Balbegno NO 639730
The Middletons bought the Woods' L-plan tower in the late seventeenth century. Now empty, it is entered through the adjoining house and a rib-vaulted hall. A watch chamber is dated 1569 with the names of I. Wood and E. Irvine.

Balmakewan NO 666663
There are scanty remains of a castle near the mansion.

Balmoral NO 255952
The holiday home of Queen Victoria and Prince Albert, built in 1855, replaced a Gordon tower of about 1550 with a round tower at one corner.

Benholm NO 804705
At one corner of the ruined mansion is a badly cracked fifteenth-century tower house built by the Ogilvies but long a seat of relatives of the Keith Earls Marischal.

Birse NO 520905
The Bishop of Aberdeen's hunting lodge of about 1600 in Birse Forest is a tower with a round stair turret surmounted by a square caphouse. It was restored and extended in about 1900.

Braemar NO 156924 (P)
The L-plan tower house, with a round stair turret in the re-entrant angle, was begun in 1628 by the Erskine Earl of Mar to provide a strongpoint against the Farquharsons. John Farquharson, the Black Colonel, burnt it in 1689, and his descendants later became the owners, although the castle was not repaired until 1748, when it was leased to the government for housing a peace-keeping garrison. The tower was then surrounded with a star-shaped chemise wall and later had its bartizans heightened into their present ugly form. It has been a Farquharson residence since the early 1800s.

Caddam NO 658685
Three dormer pediments from the former Barclay castle

remain in the wall of the steading and bear the date 1571 and the initials AB, and IS and IB.

Castle Maud NO 624995

Hidden in a clump of trees are the base of a small early tower house and a small courtyard containing outbuildings.

Cluny Crichton NO 686997

George Crichton's L-plan house, with three square rooms on each of three storeys and with shotholes around the doorway, dates from as late as 1666. It was later held by Douglases.

Corse NJ 548074

The L-plan ruin with two round turrets bears the date 1581 and the initials of William Forbes, who declared after a raid on a previous house that 'If God spares my life I shall build a house at which thieves will knock ere they enter'.

Coull NJ 513023

South of the church are the scanty remains of the castle of Alan Durward, Regent for the young Alexander III in the 1250s. It had a pentagonal enclosure with a twin-towered gateway, a hall block opposite, a round keep and at least one other round tower. Excavations conducted in 1923 suggested it was damaged in 1297, repaired about 1303 and finally destroyed during the Bruce campaign of 1307-8.

Cowie NO 887774

A motte near the ruined church bears traces of walling.

Crathes NO 734968 (NT)

The L-plan tower of the Burnetts of Leys still has its yett and bears the dates 1553 and 1596 with the monogram of Alexander Burnett and Jean Gordon. There is an array of bartizans and dormer windows at the top and one round stair turret is squared off at the top to form a clock turret and lookout platform. A later wing was destroyed by fire in the twentieth century. There are extensive fine gardens.

Dunnottar NO 882839

This fine defensive site on the coast near Stonehaven was used at an early date and was involved in the Wars of Independence. However, the earliest building now on the rock is a modest L-plan tower built by Sir William Keith in the 1390s. The rock was then consecrated ground and he was excommunicated by the Bishop of St Andrews, although this was lifted when he built a new church further inland.

In a licence of 1531 the castle is described as 'one of the

principall strengthis of our realme'. It was captured by the Catholic nobles in their rebellion of 1594, only three years after they had submitted within it to James VI. Dunnottar was then the chief residence of the Keith Earls Marischal and the large flat summit of the rock is covered with an assortment of low and plain buildings of the sixteenth and seventeenth centuries. The main apartments are set around a court and a wing attached to them containing the Earl's private suite is dated 1645. In the cellar below one hundred and twenty-two men and forty-five women Covenanters were confined under terrible conditions for two months during the summer of 1685. Only a few decades before the castle had been a Covenant stronghold protecting the Earl Marischal from Montrose. It was surrendered to Cromwell's forces in May 1652 after an eight-month siege, during which the Crown Jewels of King King Charles II were smuggled out of it into hiding below the floor of Kinneff church, where they remained until 1660. The castle was held for the government in 1689 but the tenth Earl was forfeited for his part in the 1715 Jacobite rebellion and the castle was sold and dismantled.

Durris NO 799968 and 779968
   The Frasers' courtyard castle with corner towers, replacing a Comyn motte a mile away by the Dee, was, except for some cellars, itself replaced by an L-plan tower of 1620, now attached to a modern mansion. Montrose burnt it in 1645.

Easter Clunie NO 624914
   A fragment remains beside the farm steading.

Fetteresso NO 843855
   This was the second seat of the Keith Earl Marischal and is where James Stewart was entertained at Christmas 1715. Although there was a castle here from an early period the oldest existing parts are seventeenth-century cellars. It was rebuilt in 1671 and additions were made by Admiral Duff and his son in 1782 and 1808. Though refurbished in 1947, it is now a total ruin.

Fiddes NO 805813
   The charming turreted late sixteenth-century L-plan castle of the Arbuthnotts was restored in the 1960s.

Glenbervie NO 769805
   The house incorporates the lower part of a castle built by the Douglases in the 1490s. It consists of a rectangular block set across the neck of a promontory, with round towers furnished with gunports on the landward corners. In 1572 it was besieged by Sir Adam Gordon, whose cavalry surprised a relieving force being gathered at Brechin by the Regent Mar.

Hallgreen NO 832721
The lower part of the Raits' L-plan castle of about 1600-20 is incorporated into a derelict mansion overlooking the sea.

Inglismaldie NO 644669
The altered late sixteenth-century L-plan tower of the Livingstones has three turrets on the south side and later extensions to the north-west. It passed in 1635 to Sir John Carnegie, and in 1693 to David Falconer of Newton.

Kincardine NO 671751
Among trees are remains of a square courtyard with a twin-towered gateway on the south, a hall on the east and other apartments, all probably built for Alexander II about 1220-40.

Kincausie NO 863000
The mansion includes the Irvines' sixteenth-century tower.

Kindrochit NO 152913
By the ravine of the Clunie in Braemar village are the remains of Robert II's enormous palace house with square corner towers. In 1390 it was granted to Sir Malcolm Drummond, who removed part of it to make room for a large new tower house. In 1404, while supervising work on it, he was kidnapped by Highland caterans and died in captivity. The castle was ruined by 1618 and was excavated in the 1920s.

Kirkside NO 738637
The Georgian mansion contains parts of a castle dated 16?? with the initials AS (Stratton) and EM.

Knock NJ 352952
This small ruined tower was built about 1600 by the Gordons.

Lauriston NO 759666
All that remains of the Strattons' strongly sited courtyard castle is a length of walling with a tower at each end, one being a seventeenth-century replacement of the original tower house.

Lumphanan NJ 576037
The large but low motte with a former wet moat was held by the Durwards in the thirteenth century. It bears traces of a later stone house used until the eighteenth century.

Migvie NJ 437068
Only the barest traces survive of a mid thirteenth-century courtyard castle of William, Earl of Mar, probably destroyed by the Bruces in 1307-8 and never restored.

Monboddo NO 744783
The Irvines' house has bartizans and bears the date 1635. It later passed to the Burnetts, was restored in the 1970s and now stands in the middle of a modern housing estate.

Muchalls NO 892908 (P)
The L-plan house with a courtyard and gateway was begun by Alexander Burnett in 1619 and finished by his son in 1627, the year after he was made a baronet of Nova Scotia. Possibly part of a Fraser house was included. Inside are very fine plastered' ceilings and an overmantel dated 1624.

Pitarrow NO 728750
The Wisharts' castle, birthplace of the Protestant martyr George Wishart, was demolished in 1802 but on the farmhouse are stones with the dates 1599 and 1679.

Thornton NO 688718
The Strachans' L-plan tower has one round tower dated 1531 surviving from its barmkin. Joining the two is a range dated 1662. In 1893 the estate returned to the Thorntons.

Tilquhillie NO 722741
This fine empty specimen of a Z-plan castle with two rectangular wings was begun in 1576 by John Douglas.

Whistleberry NO 862753
Only a fragment and foundations remain on a clifftop.

MORAY DISTRICT

Asliesk NJ 108598
Although a drawing of 1799 shows it complete, only a small part of this late castle of the Innes family now survives.

Auchindoun NJ 348374 (AM*)
The L-plan tower with a rib vault over the hall was built for his own use by James III's unpopular favourite Robert Cochrane, a master mason. The jealous nobles hanged him from Lauder Bridge in 1482 and Auchindoun went to the Ogilvies and then in 1535 to the Gordons. They added the rectangular court with a round tower and two ranges of offices.

Ballindalloch NJ 178365
The Grants' castle bears the date 1546, though this seems early for the Z-plan layout, with two round towers at diagonally opposite corners and a third round stair tower in the middle of one side. This stair tower was given a square caphouse in 1602 by Patrick Grant and extensive other additions and alterations were

made in the eighteenth and nineteenth centuries. The castle was captured by James Gordon in 1590 and was burnt by Montrose in 1645.

Balvenie NJ 326408 (AM)

Originally called Mortlach, this was a thirteenth-century Comyn courtyard castle with round corner towers. The towers were removed when the Douglases restored the building long after destruction in 1308 by the Bruces. It was forfeited in 1455 and held by the Stewarts until 1610, before going to the Inneses, the Forbeses and the Duffs. John Stewart, fourth Earl of Atholl, added new apartments with a round corner tower and a gateway below in the late sixteenth century. Balvenie was occupied by the Jacobites in 1689 but in 1715 William Duff fortified the castle against them. It was not inhabited after his suicide within it in 1718, though a government force briefly occupied it in 1746.

Blairfindy NJ 199286

The ruined L-plan tower, with a wing flanking two sides and a machicolation projecting above the entrance, is dated 1586 with the initials of John Gordon and his wife.

Blervie NJ 071573

A five-storey tower is the main surviving part of a Z-plan castle. A fireplace is dated 1598 with the Dunbar arms.

Brodie NH 980578 (NT)

Alexander Brodie's much altered Z-plan castle, with two square towers bearing the date 1567 and the name of the master mason, J. Russal, had a wing added in the early 1600s and is now incorporated in a mansion of the 1820s. It was burnt by the Royalist Lord Lewis Gordon in 1645.

Burgie NJ 094593

This Z-planned castle, with a fireplace dated 1602 with the Dunbar arms, is, like its twin Blervie, reduced to one very lofty tower and parts of the main block. It was mostly demolished in 1802 to provide materials for Burgie House.

Coxton NJ 262607

In front of the modern mansion is an empty little square tower bearing the Innes arms and the date 1644. It is quite strong, having vaults over all four storeys and round and square bartizans with machicolations and shotholes.

Crombie NJ 591522

The empty L-plan tower was built either by James Innes, killed at Pinkie in 1547, or Alexander Innes, outlawed for killing a kinsman in 1580. Later, John Innes was also outlawed for striking the kirk officer of Aberchirder.

Cullen NJ 507663

Sir Walter Ogilvie built the L-plan tower about 1600 as an alternative to the inconveniently sited Findlater Castle. Additions were made in the eighteenth century and 1861 and it is now owned by the Ogilvie-Grant Earl of Seafield.

Darnaway NH 994550

The castle was founded by Thomas Randolph, Earl of Moray and Regent for the young David II, but virtually the only part to survive a rebuilding of 1810 was the magnificent open roof of a hall block begun by Archibald Douglas, Earl of Moray, and finished by James II after 1455. It was later held by Queen Mary's half-brother James, Earl of Moray.

Deskford NJ 509617

Muckle House by the church appears to contain ancient work. The ruin in the garden was a part of the church.

Drumin NJ 184303

Above the Avon and Livet is a ruined fourteenth-century tower possibly built by Alexander Stewart, the Wolf of Badenoch. His grandson William sold it to the Gordons.

Drummuir NJ 417448

At the farm of Mains of Drummuir is an early seventeenth-century L-plan building of the Leslies, bearing a dormer pediment with the initials of one of the Duffs.

Duffus NJ 189672 (AM*)

The motte and bailey earthworks were raised in the 1140s by Freskin, Lord of Strabock, who took the name de Moravia and was the ancestor of the Earls and Dukes of Sutherland. It was rebuilt in stone by Sir Reginald Cheyne in the early fourteenth century, having a large but low two-storey hall keep on the mound and a large polygonal bailey. The domestic buildings along the north side date from after 1452, when the castle was wrecked by the Douglases. It was inhabited by the Sutherland Lord Duffus until the end of the seventeenth century. The motte has proved unable to support the weight of the keep and part of it has slid down the slope.

Dunphail NJ 007481

On a rock to the north of the mansion are three cellars of a late castle of the Dunbars standing on the site of a Comyn castle besieged in 1330 by Randolph, Earl of Moray.

Easter Elchies NJ 279444
A late L-plan Grant house is being restored in the 1980s.

Elgin NJ 212628
On Lady Hill are the last traces of a thirteenth-century keep and enclosure of a royal castle used by Edward I. In the town are several houses of the sixteenth and seventeenth centuries.

Findochty NJ 455673
On a rock are ruins of a sixteenth-century L-plan castle built by the Gordons and later held by the Ogilvies.

Gauldwell NJ 311451
On a promontory are the remains of a thirteenth-century castle of enclosure of the Freskins of Moray.

Gordon NJ 350596
Most of the huge former seat of the Dukes of Gordon was demolished in 1955 but a lofty Gordon tower house of about 1500 on a twelfth-century base has survived intact.

Gordonstoun NJ 184690
The Marquis of Huntly built a tall tower house in about 1620. This was replaced by a new block in 1729 although a pair of slightly later wings has survived. It later passed to the Gordon-Cummings and is now a famous public school.

Inaltry NJ 518631
Just a length of the wall of the courtyard now remains.

Innes NJ 278649
This remarkable L-plan house with fine classical details was built for Sir Robert Innes between 1640 and 1653. It later was sold to the Duff second Earl of Fife.

Kilmaichlie NJ 181321
The early seventeenth-century T-plan house of the Stewarts was sold to the Grants in the eighteenth century.

Kininvie NJ 319441
Adjoining the modern mansion is a Leslie sixteenth-century tower with a round turret crowned by a square caphouse.

Letterfourie NJ 447625
The mansion of 1776 probably incorporates a Gordon tower.

Leuchars NJ 260649
The mansion bears a stone from the former castle with the date 1583 and the Innes arms. An unusual dovecot has gone.

Mayen NJ 576477

The L-planned house with a round stair turret, built by the Gordons after 1612, incorporates parts of an earlier castle of the Abercrombies. It was bought in 1649 by William Halkett, Sheriff-Clerk of Banff, whose heiress married an Abernethy. A stone dated 1680 has the arms of both families. The Abernethys were forfeited about 1750 for the murder of Leith of Leith Hall and their castle passed to the Duffs. It was restored in the 1960s.

Milton Keith NJ 429512

Above the Isla at Keith is part of an Ogilvie castle which passed to the Oliphants and was abandoned in 1829.

Moy NJ 016599

Most of the house is the work of Major George Grant, cashiered from the army for surrendering Inverness too easily to Prince Charles, but there is older work at the back.

Mulben NJ 353512

The eastern part is a tower probably built by Sir John Grant about 1590-1600, while the remainder was the work of Ludovick Grant in the late seventeenth century.

Rothes NJ 277490

A single long piece of curtain walling remains of the Leslies' courtyard castle on a hill above the town.

Rothiemay NJ 554484

The mansion was demolished in 1959 when a doorway and a window grille were reset in a modest new house. The original palace house of the Abernethys, probably built about 1450, was much altered and extended by the Gordons and Duffs in later centuries. It was attacked by George Gordon of Gight in 1618 and was captured and plundered in 1644 by Montrose. It passed to the Duffs in 1741 and to the Forbeses in 1890.

Spynie NJ 231658

Spynie was the main seat of the Bishops of Moray from an early date. Most of the quadrangular palace, with the hall on the north and the chapel on the south, was the work of Bishop John de Winchester, a close friend of James II. The mighty tower house and other towers were added by David Stewart in reply to threats by the Earl of Huntly. James VI made Spynie a barony for Alexander Lindsey but it was later returned to the bishops, the last of whom died in 1688. The Earl of Huntly besieged the palace in 1645.

Tor NJ 125530

A single fragment remains of a tower house supposed to have

been built in 1400 by Sir Thomas Cumming.

Wester Elchies NJ 256431
A Grant house of various periods was destroyed in the 1970s.

Highland Region

BADENOCH AND STRATHSPEY DISTRICT

Castle Grant NJ 041302
The core of this forbidding derelict mansion is the Grants' sixteenth-century tower house of Freuchie. The square stair tower is perhaps a later addition. The name was changed to Castle Grant by the eighth laird in 1694. In the mid eighteenth century Sir Ludovick Grant doubled the width of the main block and added the low southern wings.

Castle Roy 007219
This small ruined quadrangular castle of enclosure was built by the Comyns in the thirteenth century.

Lethendry NJ 084274
By a farm is the Grant's ruined L-plan tower house.

Loch-an-Eilean NH 899079
On a tiny islet in a loch within Rothiemurchus Forest is a ruined castle comprising a tower house, hall block, guard house and a small lodging arranged around a small court. The tower was probably built by Alexander Stewart, the celebrated 'Wolf of Badenoch', an unruly son of Robert II. He obtained the Earldom of Ross by forcing the widowed heiress, Euphemia, to marry him. They lived apart and when the Bishop of Moray castigated Alexander for living openly with his mistress he took revenge by burning the town and Cathedral of Elgin in 1390. Robert III made him do penance at Perth but he held the north in fear till his death in 1394. The castle was later held by the Mackintoshes and the Gordons. It was attacked by the Jacobites after their defeat at Cromdale in 1690 but was successfully defended by the laird's wife, Grizell Mor. It was last used in 1715 when Mackintosh of Balnespick was confined in it to prevent him opposing the Jacobites. Ospreys nest in the ruin and no-one is ever allowed closer than the nearby shore of the loch.

Lochindorb NH 974364
On an island in the loch is a thirteenth-century Comyn courtyard castle with round corner towers. The outer court was added by the English after Edward I's stay in 1303. The castle was later held by Alexander Stewart and then the Douglases, being dismantled on their fall in 1455.

Muckrack NH 986251

Patrick Grant's small tower dated 1598, with a round stair turret surmounted by a square caphouse and a slightly later range and court, have been restored in the 1980s.

Ruthven NN 764997 (AM*)

The large, partly artificial mound overlooking the Spey opposite Kingussie is the site of a Comyn castle later held by Alexander Stewart as the chief fortress of his lordship of Badenoch. In 1451 it went to the Gordon Earl of Huntly and in that year was captured and 'kest doune' by John, Earl of Ross. It was rebuilt by 1459 when James II was there. A new castle was built for the fifth Earl of Huntly, being twice damaged by fire and in 1689 destroyed by the Jacobites. In 1718 what remained of it was cleared away and replaced by a government barracks for a peace-keeping force. In 1745 Sergeant Molloy and just twelve men made a gallant defence of the barracks against two hundred Jacobites. They held out and were left in peace until 1746, when after another brave defence of three days they surrendered on good terms and marched away. Later the Jacobites burnt the barracks.

CAITHNESS DISTRICT

Achastle ND 116227

On a promontory above Berriedale village and some way in front of Langwell House are traces of a small courtyard.

Ackergill ND 352547

The lofty five-storey tower was built by the Keiths in the late fifteenth century. In 1547 the Crown granted remission to George Sinclair, Earl of Caithness, for the treasonable capture and holding of the tower and for detaining its captain, Alexander Keith, in Girnigoe and Braal castles. In 1592-3 George Keith, Earl Marischal, complained to the Privy Council that his jealous brother Robert had forcibly occupied Ackergill with the intention of molesting the neighbourhood. In 1598 the Earl complained again that a kinsman, John Keith of Subster, and his two sons and others had gone by night 'and ledderit (scaled with ladders) the walls of his place at Ackergill', spoiled the castle, harmed the servants and was now keeping the tower. Later it passed to the Sinclairs and then to the Dunbars of Hempriggs. There are nineteenth-century extensions on the seaward side.

Barrogill ND 290739

Under its modern name of the Castle of Mey this building is famous as the Highland home of Queen Elizabeth the Queen Mother, who purchased it in 1952. It is a somewhat altered

Z-plan building with square towers and a courtyard and was built about 1580-1600 for William Sinclair, fourth son of George, fourth Earl of Caithness.

Berriedale ND 122224
On a rock by the mouth of the Berriedale Water are the foundations of a castle of enclosure owned in turn by the Cheynes, Sutherlands, Oliphants and Sinclairs.

Braal ND 139601
By a later mansion is a ruined fourteenth-century tower house possibly built by Alexander of Ard. It was granted to David Stewart in 1375, to Admiral Crichton in 1452, and later passed to the Sinclairs. They began the mansion, although it was not completed until the nineteenth century.

Brimms ND 043710
Remotely sited on the north coast are the derelict tiny L-plan tower and courtyard built about 1600 for the Sinclairs.

Brough ND 228741
A ditch and slight traces remain on a clifftop promontory.

Bucholly ND 383658
On a spectacular clifftop site almost isolated from the mainland, and probably occupied as early as the twelfth century, are ruins of a sixteenth-century castle of enclosure with a hall and gatehouse built by the Mowats.

Clyth ND 307386
In a rather inaccessible site on a rock by the shore are the foundations of a tower built about 1500 by the Gunns.

Dirlot ND 126486
The base of a small tower built by the Cheynes in the fourteenth century, or the Gunns in the fifteenth, lies on a rock above the river Thurso in a lonely position far inland.

Dounreay NC 983669
Because of the adjacent atomic power station the late sixteenth-century Sinclair castle is now inaccessible except by sea. The ruin remained occupied until 1861.

Dunbeath ND 158282
This inhabited clifftop castle was founded in the fifteenth century but is mostly the work of John Sinclair in the 1630s, though with considerable modern extensions and alterations. In 1650 the castle was captured by Montrose but after his defeat at

Carbisdale was retaken by General Leslie after the garrison's water supply failed.

Forse ND 224338

On a coastal headland is an early ruined tower with a sixteenth-century court and buildings behind it. It was held in turn by the Cheynes, Keiths and Sutherlands.

Girnigoe ND 379549

This spectacular coastal promontory was the chief seat of the Sinclair Earls of Caithness. A tower house of about 1500 divided a long narrow inner court, with foundations of many apartments, from an outer court, also containing apartments added by the fifth Earl and once dated 1607 on a lintel. This outer court is sometimes confusingly known under the separate name Castle Sinclair. The sixth Earl left Girnigoe to Campbell of Glenorchy in lieu of debts. The rightful heir, his cousin George Sinclair of Kiess Castle, besieged and took Girnigoe in 1679. Both castles were ruined by 1700.

Halberry ND 302377

At the neck of a coastal promontory is the base of the fifteenth-century tower house of the chief of the Gunns.

Kiess ND 357616

The small ruined clifftop Z-plan castle with two round turrets was built about 1600 by the fifth Earl of Caithness.

Knockkinnan ND 181315

On a knoll above the A9 coast road are the barest traces of a tower house and a surrounding courtyard of about 1500.

Mestag ND 340764

In an inaccessible position on top of a stack on the west side of Stroma Island is the base of a small tower.

Scrabster ND 107691

There are traces of a thirteenth-century courtyard castle of the Bishops of Caithness on a low rock west of Thurso.

Wick ND 369488

One of the oldest towers in Scotland, the Old Man of Wick is probably of the twelfth century, when Caithness and Sutherland were under Norse rule from Orkney. On the narrow promontory behind the ruin are traces of apartments of later date when the tower was held by the Cheynes and then the Oliphants. In 1569, after a brawl in Wick between feuding Oliphants and Sinclairs, lack of provisions made Lord Oliphant surrender the castle to John Sinclair, Master of Caithness, after a siege of eight days.

INVERNESS AND NAIRN DISTRICTS

Boath NH 918556 and 920558
A dovecot stands within the rampart of the ring motte of Eren erected by King William about 1180. Nearby Boath House of 1825 incorporates parts of the mansion the dovecot served.

Castle Stuart NH 741498
This castle of the Stuart Earls of Moray, with two square towers on the same side, was new in 1624, when it was forcibly occupied by the Mackintoshes, former owners of the estate.

Cawdor NH 847499 (P)
The existing castle has no connection with Macbeth, the most famous of many Thanes of Cawdor, and originated in a late fourteenth-century tower house. A licence was granted for refortification in 1454, after which the tower was surrounded by a rectangular court with a dry ditch on the three sides away from the burn. A drawbridge crosses this and there is a yett which the Thane brought from the castle of Lochindorb, which he was ordered to dismantle. The Campbells obtained Cawdor by kidnapping the infant heiress, Muriel Calder, from her Rose relatives at Kilravock and marrying her at the age of twelve to the Earl of Argyll's son Sir John Campbell in 1511. Created peers in 1796 and earls in 1829, this branch of the Campbells is still at Cawdor. The courtyard is now occupied by ranges of apartments of various centuries, mainly the seventeenth.

Culloden NH 721465
The house of 1772-83 incorporates the cellars of Duncan Forbes's house of the 1630s, destroyed by Cumberland after his victory over the Jacobites on the nearby moor in 1746.

Dalcross NH 779483
The eighth Lord Lovat's L-plan castle dated 1620 was extended by the Mackintoshes in 1703 and was restored from ruin in the twentieth century. The numerous window grilles give it an unusually authentic seventeenth-century appearance.

Erchless NH 410408
The Chisholms' extended L-plan tower of about 1600 was besieged by five hundred Jacobites in 1689 but held for them in 1715 and 1745.

Inshes NH 695437
A house of 1767 has replaced the main house or tower but one square turret dovecot with gunports remains from a court.

1. Hermitage Castle (Roxburgh District, Borders), a large tower house of the late fourteenth century with three square corner towers added about 1400.

2. Neidpath Castle (Tweeddale District, Borders), a fourteenth-century L-plan tower with a later court and outbuildings.

3. Gilnockie or Hollows Tower (Annandale and Eskdale District, Dumfries and Galloway) is a restored typical border tower.

4. Morton Castle (Nithsdale District, Dumfries and Galloway), a ruined hall block with a tower at one end.

5. Orchardton Tower (Stewartry District, Dumfries and Galloway), of about 1450, is unique in Scotland in being round inside and out.

6. (Left) Cardoness Castle (Stewartry District, Dumfries and Galloway) is a noble six-storey structure dating from about 1480 to 1510.

7. (Right) Threave Castle (Stewartry District, Dumfries and Galloway) lies on an island in the river Dee. A wall of about 1450 with round corner towers surrounds Archibald the Grim's tower of about 1370.

8. Balgonie Castle (Fife). The oldest part is a massive ashlar-faced tower house of about 1450.

9. St Andrews Castle (Fife). The Fore Tower is the much altered former gatehouse of about 1200.

10. Ravenscraig Castle (Fife), the first fortress in Britain designed for defence against artillery, was begun about 1460 but never finished.

11. Craigievar Castle (Gordon District, Grampian). The ornamental upper parts were added by the Bell family of masons in the 1620s to the late sixteenth-century lower parts.

12. (Left) Huntly Castle (Gordon District, Grampian), showing the round tower of the palace, a structure mostly of the 1550s but with an older base and top parts of about 1600-2.

13. (Below) Duffus Castle (Moray District, Grampian). The fine fourteenth-century keep lies on top of the mid twelfth-century motte.

14. *Kinkell Castle (Ross and Cromarty District, Highland) is a restored Mackenzie tower of the 1590s.*

15. Girnigoe Castle (Caithness District, Highland), a spectacular promontory site with a tower house of about 1500.

16. (Above) *Dirleton Castle (East Lothian District, Lothian), a much rebuilt thirteenth-century courtyard castle on a rock.*

17. (Right) *Tantallon Castle (East Lothian District, Lothian): the gatehouse.*

18. *Preston Tower (East Lothian District, Lothian) is an L-plan structure of about 1400 with seventeenth-century upper parts.*

19. Crichton Castle (Midlothian District, Lothian); a tower house of about 1370 adjoins a hall block of the 1440s.

20. Craigmillar Castle (Edinburgh District, Lothian) has a courtyard of the 1420s added to an L-plan tower of the 1370s.

21. Dunstaffnage Castle (Argyll and Bute District, Strathclyde) has a modest thirteenth-century courtyard set on a rock.

22. Rowallan Castle (Kilmarnock District, Strathclyde), showing the sixteenth-century gatehouse range. The base of the much older tower house lies on the right.

23. *Killochan Castle (Kyle and Carrick District, Strathclyde) is a fine L-plan building dated 1586.*

24. *Castle Menzies (Perth and Kinross District, Tayside) is a large Z-plan building with two square wings dated 1577.*

25. Elcho Castle (Perth and Kinross District, Tayside) is a fine specimen of a mid sixteenth-century mansion with various towers and turrets. It has gunports and some of the windows retain their iron grilles.

26. Huntingtower Castle (Perth and Kinross District, Tayside). A fifteenth-century tower and a sixteenth-century L-plan tower close by were joined in the seventeenth century.

Inshoch NH 936567

Behind a farm is the Hays' ruined Z-plan castle of about 1600 with two round towers. A later wing is entirely destroyed.

Inverness NH 666451

Only a well now survives of the royal castle of Inverness, which had a long illustrious history, and a mock castle of 1835 housing the Sheriff Court and County Police Department stands on the site. David I and William the Lion had here a timber castle, which was eventually superseded by a tower house and court. This would appear to have been the work of Alexander Stewart, the Earl of Mar, who in 1411 halted the invasion of the Macdonald Lord of the Isles in support of a claim to the Earldom of Ross at a very bloody battle at Harlaw. James I summoned fifty Highland chiefs, including Alexander, Lord of the Isles, to meet him at Inverness Castle in 1427. They were all imprisoned there until they gave hostages and pledges of good behaviour. The Lord of the Isles returned in 1429 and burnt the town although the castle held out. His son John became Earl of Ross in 1437. In 1455 John captured the castle during the Douglases' fight against James II. For many years he acted as a semi-independent prince but in 1476 was forced to submit to James III, losing both the Ross earldom and the Lordship of the Isles. He became a pensioner at court while his Macdonald kinsmen continued to wreak havoc for another seventy or so years.

In 1562 Queen Mary's forces captured the castle from the Gordons and hanged the keeper. Montrose failed to take it in 1644 but a party of Royalists captured it in 1649. The castle was then in a bad state and Cromwell built a citadel nearby, which Charles II had destroyed in the 1660s. The old castle was patched up by the government later and was finally captured and blown up by the Jacobites in 1746.

Kilravock NH 814493

Kilravock has been owned by the Rose family since the thirteenth century. It has a tower house of about 1460-70 linked by a stair turret to a long seventeenth-century mansion.

Moniack NH 552436

The much altered and extended early seventeenth-century L-plan castle is now the home of a Highland winery.

Moy NH 775443

Only traces remain of the Mackintoshes' island refuge.

Rait NH 894525

The Raits' ruined hall house of the fourteenth century has a round corner tower and traces of some later outbuildings.

Urquhart NH 531286

Urquhart is a large and strong fortress built on a rock on the north side of Loch Ness. The small, irregularly shaped enclosure on the highest part of the site was built by Alan Durward in the mid thirteenth century and the large main courtyard of hourglass shape was created in the late thirteenth and fourteenth centuries. In it are a much ruined substantial range of domestic apartments.

As a key fortress, Urquhart was garrisoned in 1296 by Edward I's forces, who soon found themselves hard pressed by the Scots when the English king retreated south again. After two attacks the castle fell and when Edward came north again in 1303 it had to be recaptured, requiring a long siege. In 1333 the castle was one of six which held out for David II against Edward Balliol and Edward III of England.

The castle reverted to the Crown in 1346 and remained royal until capture in the 1450s by the Earl of Ross. After his downfall it was handed over in 1476 to the Earl of Huntly. However, not even the Gordons could stop the depredations of the Macdonalds and in 1509 James IV gave the castle to John Grant of Freuchie on condition that he 'repair or build at the castle a tower, with an outwork or rampart of stone and lime, for protecting the lands and people from the inroads of thieves and malefactors; to construct requisite offices, such as a pantry, bakehouse, brewhouse, oxhouse, kiln, cot, dovegrove, and orchard, with the necessary fences'. The Grants appear to have implemented this almost to the word and the gatehouse, most of the tower house and the present courtyard walls are their work. However, the Macdonalds still succeeded in capturing the castle in about 1515 and 1545 and devastated it and the surrounding area.

At Christmas 1644 Lady Urquhart was raided by a force of Covenanters, who completely sacked the castle but left her in possession. The castle held out against six hundred Jacobites in 1689 but was dismantled later to prevent them using it.

LOCHABER DISTRICT

Ardtornish NM 692426

Overlooking the Sound of Mull are the remains of a thirteenth-century hall house, where in 1461 the Lord of the Isles and Earl of Ross signed the extraordinary treaty of 'Westminster-Ardtornish' by which he, the Earl of Douglas and Edward IV proposed to divide Scotland between them.

Caisteal Dubh Nan Cliar NM 473631

On a rock are the remains of a tiny tower of late date which was probably an outpost of Mingary Castle.

Glensanda NM 824469

Overlooking Loch Linnhe is a ruined fifteenth-century tower of just two storeys with an attic in the gables.

Invergarry NM 315006

This castle is a lofty L-planned, mid seventeenth-century ruin standing on a cliff above Loch Oich. After the revolution of 1688 Alastair Macdonald of Glengarry fortified it for the deposed James VII (II of England) and with impunity received James's envoys here. The castle was difficult for government forces to reach, especially with the cannon required to batter it into submission. In the event Glengarry and the other neighbouring chiefs made their submission to the government of William III after the dreadful massacre of the inhabitants of Glencoe in 1692.

The castle was back in Macdonald hands during the 1745-6 rebellion and was twice visited by Prince Charles. Afterwards it was burned and probably dismantled by Cumberland.

Inverlochy NN 120754

The ruined castle built about 1270-80 by the Comyn Lord of Badenoch lies on flat ground beside the Lochy near Fort William. It has a quadrangular court with a round tower at each corner, one being bigger than the others to form a keep or residence for the lord. There were two entrances, opposite each other, which were closed by portcullises. The Comyns were destroyed by Robert Bruce and Inverlochy was later held by the Gordons of Huntly. Alongside the castle were fought two important battles, in 1431 and 1645. In the first Donald Balloch and Alasdair Carrach led the Macdonalds to victory over a junior branch of the royal Stewarts, the Earl of Caithness being among those killed. In the second Montrose led the Highlanders to victory over the Covenant forces of his deadly enemy the Campbell Marquis of Argyll.

Kinlochaline NM 697476

The Macleans' fifteenth-century tower on a rock was captured by the royalist Macdonalds in 1644. It was abandoned about 1690, restored about 1890, and now lies empty.

Mingary NM 502631

The small hexagonal thirteenth-century castle of enclosure contains ruined eighteenth-century lodgings erected by the Campbells or Murrays. At the time of two visits to it by James IV it was owned by the MacIans of Ardnamurchan and they were besieged in it by the Macdonalds in 1515 and again, more successfully, in 1517. The Macleans, with Spanish aid, failed to take it in 1588 but the castle was captured in 1644 by Alasdair

Macdonald by means of setting up a fire outside the gate. General Leslie retook it in 1647.

Tioram NM 663725
This small and remotely sited pentagonal thirteenth-century castle of enclosure containing later domestic buildings was the home in the 1350s of Amie, the estranged wife of John, Lord of the Isles. Her Macdonald descendants inhabited the castle until it was burnt out in 1715.

Tor NN 133786
The massive but very ruinous tower on a cliff above the Lochy was probably built by Alasdair Carrach between 1380 and 1440. In the early sixteenth century it was inhabited and rebuilt by the Camerons in the face of opposition from the Keppoch Macdonalds. A younger branch of the Cameron chief's family used it until the early eighteenth century.

ROSS AND CROMARTY DISTRICT

Arkendeith NH 695561
Beside a farmhouse high above Avoch on the Black Isle is a fragment of a late tower of the Bruces of Kinloss.

Ballone NH 929837
Roderick Mackenzie's ruined Z-plan castle, with one round tower and one square one, lies overlooking the North Sea.

Balnagown NH 763752
The castle held by the Ross family from 1371 until 1711 has been greatly altered and extended by later owners. It was reported to the Privy Council in 1569 that Alexander, the eighth laird, had so 'herreit and wrakkit' neighbouring Crown tenants that they were unable to pay their rents.

Cadboll NH 879776
A farmhouse adjoins the Denoons' ruined sixteenth-century L-plan castle with a round tower on the outermost corner.

Castle Leod NH 485593
The date 1616 and the initials of Roderick Mackenzie and Margaret Macleod, ancestors of the present owner, the Earl of Cromartie, refer to additions to an L-plan tower of about 1580.

Castle Craig NH 632638
Above the northern shore of the Black Isle is a sixteenth-century castle of the Bishops of Ross with an L-plan tower standing at a landward facing corner of a square courtyard.

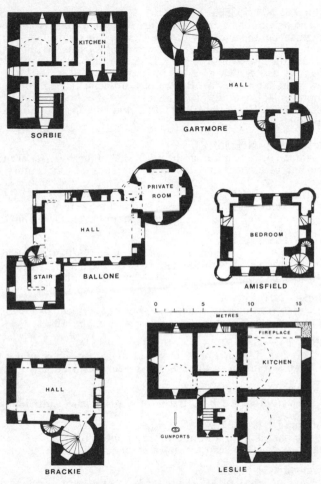

Fig. 3. Sixteenth and seventeenth century castles. Amisfield Tower (Nithsdale District) mostly of about 1600, has round bartizans containing closets opening off the top bedroom. Brackie Castle (Angus District) and Sorbie Castle (Wigtown District) are L-planned towers of the 1580s and 1590s with the wing used to contain a wide stair. Leslie Castle (Gordon District) dating from the 1660s, is an L-plan with the stair in an additional turret set within the re-entrant angle. Gartmore Castle (Stirling District) and Ballone Castle (Ross and Cromarty District) are Z-plan castles of about 1580 and about 1620 respectively.

Dingwall NH 553589
The only remains of the castle are three shapeless ivy-mantled fragments in the garden of Castle House. The original earth and timber motte and bailey castle was built by King William the Lion in the late twelfth century. Later the Earls of Ross rebuilt it in stone. James IV had a hall built after his visit of 1503 and, a few years later, Andro, Bishop of Caithness, carried out some improvements on it after assaults by the Macdonalds and Mackenzies. It was decayed by 1625 and later dismantled for its materials.

Dochmaluag NH 521601
Hidden in vegetation on the north side of Strathpeffer are the remains of an L-plan building of the seventeenth century.

Fairburn NH 469523
The Mackenzies' square early sixteenth-century tower was heightened and given a projecting stair turret about 1600.

Kilcoy NH 576512
This Z-plan Mackenzie castle of about 1620-30, with two round towers and with the date 1679 on the hall fireplace, was restored from ruin in the early twentieth century.

Kinkell NH 554543
The tower house of the Mackenzies of Gairloch, dated 1594, with a round stair turret, was restored in the 1960s.

Little Tarrel NH 911819
This low L-plan house of about 1600, with big gunports, became a ruin but in the 1980s it is being restored as a home.

Lochslin NH 849806
On a hilltop are bare traces of a tower and outbuildings.

Newmore NH 680719
The basement of a Munro tower of about 1625, with a round stair turret, lies in a garden. It was later held by the Mackenzies.

Ormond NH 696536
On a hill south of Avoch are the barest traces of a rectangular courtyard with square corner towers, probably built by William the Lion about 1200-14. It was later owned by the Regent Sir Andrew Moray, who died there about 1338, and then went in turn to the Douglases and a brother of James IV, who took from it the title of Earl of Ormond.

Redcastle NH 584495
Most of the present L-planned mansion is the work of the

Mackenzies, who owned it from 1570 to 1790, and it bears the initials of Roderick Mackenzie and the date 1641. However, the thick walls overlooking the ravine are the last relics of a tower house and courtyard built by the Douglases in the fourteenth and fifteenth centuries, and it stands on the site of William the Lion's timber castle of Edradour built in 1179. The building became derelict after being used to accommodate troops in the Second World War.

Shandwick NH 787754
North of the Ross family's present mansion is a derelict eighteenth-century house with older parts round the back.

Strome NG 862354 (NT*)
On a headland by the former ferry point is a courtyard built by the Macdonalds of Glengarry, probably in the fifteenth century, and destroyed by the Mackenzies in 1590.

Tulloch NH 547605
The sixteenth-century tower of the Bainses passed to the Davidsons in 1760. It now stands in a much altered state at one corner of a mansion of several periods used as an academy.

SKYE AND LOCHALSH DISTRICT

Brochel NG 584463
On a high rock at the north end of the island of Raasay is a small ruined castle built about 1500 by the Macleods.

Caisteal Maoil NG 758264
On a high rock at the ferry crossing from Kyle of Lochalsh to Skye is a shattered fifteenth-century tower.

Caisteal Uisdean NG 381583
This fifteenth-century ruin lies on the west side of Trotternish. The name refers to Hugh, a sixteenth-century owner of it. It was a tower apparently of just two storeys.

Dunscaith NG 595121
On a low headland on the north side of Sleat are remnants of a courtyard castle which was the original seat of the Macdonalds of Sleat before they transferred to Duntulm.

Duntulm NG 410743
The original tower house and courtyard date from around 1540, when James V anchored in the bay below and received the submission of the chiefs of Skye. However, much of the present ruin on a headland at the north end of Trotternish dates from

about 1611. In that year the Privy Council ordained that 'the said Sir Donald (Macdonald of Sleat) sall mak his residence and duelling at Duntillum and yf he has not a sufficient comlie house ansuerable to his estate already thair he sall with all convenient diligence, prepair materials and caus build an civile and comlie house and if his house be decayed he sall repair the same'.

Dunvegan NG 247481 (P)

Leod's castle of about 1270 on a rock on the west side of Skye has remained continuously occupied ever since by his descendants, the chiefs of Macleod. Not much of the original wall of enclosure now survives, having been replaced on the landward side by buildings of several centuries and on the other side cut down to courtyard level to give a nineteenth-century chief a seaward view. The massive tower added in the late fourteenth century by Malcolm, third chief, has a projecting turret with an unpleasant pit prison in its base. Alistair Crotach added the Fairy Tower at the south-east corner about 1500 and between the two towers was the original hall, though the present range here dates from the seventeenth century and was much remodelled in the eighteenth and nineteenth centuries. The south range was added by Ian Breac in 1684-90 while the north range was added by Major-General Norman Macleod, twenty-third chief, and was intended originally to house part of the second battalion Black Watch, which he was then raising from among his tenants. John Norman, twenty-fourth chief, and his son Norman transformed the castle, adding the existing entrance to replace the old sea-gate, a top storey to the east range, corridors of access to pull together the haphazardly planned building as a unit, and the tiny ornamental bartizans and present battlements.

Eilean Donan NG 881259 (P)

This famous castle stands on an islet close to the shore of Loch Duich near Dornie. Alexander II's original castle of about 1220 had a small rectangular courtyard similar to Castle Roy. In the fourteenth century the Mackenzies added a large and massive tower house in one corner. They later transferred their main attention from Kintail to the richer lands of Easter Ross and they left the MacRaes in charge of the castle. They defended it against various assaults by the Macdonalds and in 1539, during one of these, Donald Gorm of Sleat was mortally wounded by an arrow shot from it. The Macraes added a block in the corner opposite that from the tower, and a polygonal cistern bastion facing the approach. In 1719 the castle was bombarded and wrecked by three English frigates to dislodge some Jacobites. Thus most of the masonry now visible is the work of Colonel John Macrae, who restored the shattered ruin between 1912 and 1932.

Knock NG 672087
On a headland on the south side of Sleat are fragments of what may be a thirteenth-century hall house. Donald Gorm of Sleat was confirmed in possession of it (then called Castle Camus) in 1614 and a thinly walled wing was added later.

SUTHERLAND DISTRICT

Ardvreck NC 240236
The wreck of a square tower with a round stair turret built about 1600 by the Macleods of Assynt lies on the neck of a peninsula in the loch. Montrose took refuge with Neil Macleod here in 1650 but was betrayed to the Covenant authorities and subsequently executed in Edinburgh. The castle was destroyed in 1672 during the last of three raids made in retribution by the Mackenzies. It was replaced by Calda House nearby, itself burnt by the Macraes in 1760, and left a ruin.

Borve NC 725642
On a promontory on the lonely north coast are the last traces of the Mackays' tower house and courtyard.

Caisteal Bharraich NC 581567
This tiny tower was used by the Bishops of Caithness when in transit between Scrabster Castle and Balnakiel House.

Caisteal Na Coire NC 466012
The base of a tower house stands by the river Oykell.

Dornoch NH 797897
The original Bishop's Palace was burnt in 1570 during a feud between the Murrays of Dornoch and Mackays of Strathnaver. It was replaced by the present L-plan building which was once used as a prison and is now a hotel.

Dunrobin NC 850008 (P)
The Freskin Earls of Sutherland had a castle here in the thirteenth century, but the present home of the Duchess of Sutherland comprises the Gordon Earl of Sutherland's sixteenth-century tower and a seventeenth-century courtyard mansion with round corner turrets, almost engulfed by the nineteenth-century extensions of the Leveson-Gower Dukes.

Helmsdale ND 027151
A tourist office stands on the site of a hunting lodge of the Sutherlands built in 1488 and rebuilt in 1616. Here in 1567 Isobel Sinclair poisoned John, eleventh Earl, and his wife, hoping to divert the succession to her own son, who, however, was poisoned whilst the rightful heir escaped.

Invershin NH 573964
Only the barest traces of this castle remain by the Oykell.

Proncy NH 772926
The base of a tower house lies on a circular platform.

Skelbo NH 792952
By Loch Fleet are a fourteenth-century hall keep and a later courtyard of a Sutherland castle on the end of a ridge.

Lothian Region

EAST LOTHIAN DISTRICT

Auldhame NT 602847
One long ruined wall with various projections remains of a sixteenth-century mansion on the cliff south of Tantallon.

Ballencrieff NT 487783
The house of John Murray, first Lord Elibank, built about 1600-25, was given a north front and a new east end about 1730. It has been a ruin since a fire in 1868.

Barnes NT 528766
This large symmetrical mansion and forecourt with square towers and shotholes was begun by Sir John Seton, Treasurer of the Household and Extraordinary Lord of Session under James VI. It was left incomplete at his death in 1594.

Bass NT 601873
This huge volcanic plug rising 300 feet (90 m) above the sea has the only access to its summit blocked by a long curtain wall of the sixteenth century and later, although the rock was a refuge and prison long before then. In the 1650s it menaced Cromwell's supply ships with its big guns. The Bass was sold to the Crown in 1671 and used as a prison for Covenanters. In 1691 four imprisoned Jacobite officers took the place over and held it for the exiled King James VII for nearly three years. It was dismantled in 1701 but repaired when a lighthouse was built on the wall in 1902.

Dirleton NT 518841 (AM)
The original de Vaux castle had a compact courtyard on a rock with three large round towers, one of which combined with two other projections to form an unusual type of citadel at the south-west corner. The castle was captured by the English in 1298 and held by them until 1311, when it was captured and

destroyed by Bruce's forces.

In the fourteenth and fifteenth centuries the Hallyburtons replaced the demolished eastern towers with a very massive hall block. The castle passed in 1515 to the Ruthvens, who later built the part of the citadel facing the main court. After their forfeiture in 1600, it was held in turn by the Earl of Kellie, Sir James Douglas, James Maxwell and the Nesbits. The castle was not used again after 1651, when Major General Lambert captured it after a brief bombardment.

Dunbar NT 678794

The Earls of Dunbar had a castle here, over which a battle was fought between the Scots and the English in 1297. Black Agnes, Countess of Dunbar, held it against the Earl of Salisbury in 1338. Parliament ordered it destroyed in 1488 to deny its use to the English or Scots rebels, but a decade later James IV was rebuilding it. Fragments and foundations and a ruined block house added by John, Duke of Albany, about 1515 stand on two rocks by the harbour. Further fortifications added by the French in 1560 were destroyed under the terms of the Treaty of Leith the same year. Queen Mary fled here after Riccio's murder and was brought here after her abduction by the Earl of Bothwell, then its keeper. Afterwards Parliament again ordered the castle to be destroyed.

Elphinstone NT 391698

Sir Gilbert Johnstone's fine fifteenth-century tower, with an exceptional number of mural chambers and stairs, stood complete until 1955, when mining subsidence resulted in it being destroyed to basement level.

Falside NT 378710

To a fifteenth-century tower with a top vault has been added an L-planned extension with bartizans bearing the date 1618 on a dormer window, with the initials of John Falside and his wife. It was restored from ruin in the 1970s.

Fenton NT 543822

This ruined L-plan building has a stair turret projecting from the back wall, level with the crosswall. It bore the date 1577 with the initials of Sir John Carmichael, Warden of the Scottish Middle March, murdered by borderers in 1600.

Fountainhall NT 427677

A small sixteenth-century house called Woodhead was given an extension dated 1638 with John Pringle's initials. The name was changed after purchase in 1685 by John Lauder of Newington, for whom further additions were made.

Gamelshiel NT 649648

Only a fragment remains of this small late tower house.

Garleton NT 509767

Sir John Seton's sixteenth-century castle has a very ruinous block with a round tower and a court with two out-houses at the far corners, the southern one being a kitchen.

Hailes NT 575758 (AM)

It was probably Sir Patrick Hepburn, who played a valiant part in the battle of Otterburn in 1388, who extended a modest thirteenth-century courtyard castle of the Earls of Dunbar, adding a tower house. In 1400 the Earl of March and Hotspur Percy failed to take it by assault and were themselves surprised and routed after dark by the Master of Douglas. Archibald Dunbar captured the castle in 1443 and 'slew them that he found thairin'. It was burnt in 1532 and in 1547 was occupied by Lord Grey of Wilton, who reported it as being strong and well furnished. Later owners were Queen Mary's lover Bothwell, Hercules Stewart, and the Setons, who in 1700 sold the castle to Lord Hailes.

Innerwick NT 735737

A series of vaults of the fifteenth and sixteenth centuries occupies the top of a rock overlooking the Thornton Burn. The castle was built by the Stewarts and Hamiltons and in 1547 the English smoked the garrison into submission and dismantled it.

Johnscleugh NT 631665

The house is probably adapted from a small tower house.

Keith Marischal NT 449643

The Keith Earl Marischal's L-plan house of 1589 has been somewhat remodelled and added to in later centuries.

Kilspindie NT 462801

A fragment remains of 'the castell toure and fortalice biggit by Patrick Douglas', granted to Alexander Hay in 1612.

Lennoxlove NT 515721 (P)

The large fifteenth-century L-plan tower was the home of the Maitlands, one of whom was Queen Mary's secretary. The tower was burnt by the English in 1549 and was altered and extended by John Maitland, created Earl of Lauderdale in 1640. The name was changed from Lethington to Lennoxlove under the will of the Duchess of Lennox who died in 1703. It is now the home of the Duke and Duchess of Hamilton.

Luffness NT 476804

The T-plan castle bears the date 1584 and the initials of Patrick Hepburn. A small earlier tower would appear to be incorporated and there are later additions and alterations. Around it are traces of a fort built by the French in 1549, destroyed under the terms of the Treaty of Leith in 1560.

Markle NT 579775

The ruin comprises two modest adjacent ranges and traces of a small square courtyard. It was burnt in 1401 and 1544.

Monkton NT 349717

The small tower of about 1550 of the Hays of Yester was extended with an L-plan range, a court and other buildings. With their forfeiture in 1746, the house went to the Falconers.

Northfield NT 390739

Joseph Marjoribanks' L-plan house of 1611 has bartizans.

Nunraw NT 597706

Incorporated in the mansion of 1860 is the much altered Z-plan castle of the Hepburns, with two square flanking towers.

Ormiston NT 413677

Old cellars remain in the office court of the later hall.

Penshiel NT 642632

A ruined oblong block survives of this monastic grange.

Preston NT 393742

The Hamiltons' early fifteenth-century L-plan tower was burnt by Hertford in 1544 and was extended upwards by two storeys within the original parapet in 1626. Dormers on the later work have the initials of Sir John and Dame Katherine Hamilton. The tower was burnt by Cromwell's forces in 1650 and again accidentally in 1663 after being restored.

Redhouse NT 463771

John Laing's house of about 1600 consists of a court with an office range on the east and the main apartments on the north. The latter were widened, shortened and made into a tower soon after by Sir Andrew Hamilton. It has been a ruin since the Jacobite George Hamilton was forfeited in 1746.

Saltcoats NT 486819

A cottage adjoining the ruin had a panel with the date 1390 (a mistake for 1590) and the initials of Sir Patrick Livingstone and Margaret Fawside. Their castle has a court with a house along one side, with at one end a pair of round turrets which are corbelled out into squares and linked at the top by an arch. Saltcoats passed to the Hamiltons in the eighteenth century and was dismantled for materials about 1810.

Seacliffe NT 612844
There are slight remains on a low headland above the sea.

Stoneypath NT 596714
On a promontory is the ruined fifteenth-century tower of the Lyles, later held by the Douglases.

Tantallon NT 596851 (AM)
Built about 1370, William, Earl of Douglas's castle was one of the strongest in Scotland. The inner court has sheer cliffs on three sides, while the fourth, facing an outer court, has a ditch and a wall 12 feet (3.7 m) thick and 50 feet (15 m) high with a round tower at either end and a central gatehouse containing lordly apartments. A hall and other apartments lie within.

After the treasonable contact of the fifth Earl of Angus with the English court, Tantallon was besieged by James IV in 1491, although the two were reconciled in 1492. The next Earl married the King's widow, Margaret Tudor. James V turned against his stepfather and in 1528 battered away at the walls of Tantallon without effect and on retreating lost part of his artillery to a surprise attack. The King took over the castle on the Earl's exile in 1529 and had it strengthened. The Earl returned only after James's death in 1542. The castle was yielded to the Covenanters in 1639 as it was without a proper garrison, and in 1651 it was captured by General Monck from a troop of Royalist cavalry that was raiding Cromwell's lines of communication with England. The castle decayed after it was sold to Hew Dalrymple in 1699.

Tranent NT 404729
A ruined sixteenth-century L-plan tower stands beside a modern house in Church Street in the town.

Waughton NT 567809
Only a ruined wing remains of a sixteenth-century L-plan house and courtyard on a low rocky platform.

Whitekirk NT 595816
The barn-like building north-west of the church is Oliver Sinclair's tower of about 1540, burnt by the English in 1544 amd 1548, and later extended with a long gabled roof.

Whittinghame NT 602733
The Douglases' modest L-plan tower has a gun platform and

later extensions. It passed in 1660 to Lord Kingston.

Woodhall NT 433680
The house includes a small altered tower of the Sinclairs.

Yester NT 556667
On a strong promontory site are the ruins of the Giffards' courtyard castle built in 1268, occupied by the English in 1311, and captured and recaptured in the late 1540s. Under the wall are a remarkable subterranean chamber, called the Goblin Hall, with a ribbed vault, and a postern and well.

MIDLOTHIAN AND EDINBURGH CITY DISTRICTS

Bavelaw NT 168628
This small L-plan building, probably of about 1600, was restored from ruin in the early nineteenth century and extended about 1900. In 1628 it was granted to the advocate Laurence Scott.

Borthwick NT 370597
This 80 foot (24 m) high tower house with two wings, both on the same side, is one of the strongest and best appointed medieval towers in Britain. Sir William Borthwick was licensed to build it in 1430. Because it has a top vault as well as others directly below and above the great hall, it was almost fireproof, and its six storeys (eight in the wings) contain a large number of rooms. Surrounding the tower is a wedge-shaped courtyard with a large round tower at the corner by the entrance. The large scar on the east side of the tower and the subsequent rebuilding of the parapet on this side without the machicolations are attributed to a battering by Cromwell, Lord Borthwick having defied him in 1650.

Brunstane NT 201582
The ruin comprises a house with a square stair turret and a courtyard with a square corner tower flanking the entrance. Though attributed to Alexander Crichton, attainted in 1554, it bears the date 1568 and the initials of his son.

Cakemuir NT 413591
Adam Wauchope's mid sixteenth-century tower, with a semi-circular stair turret with a rectangular caphouse, was extended in 1761 and restored in the nineteenth century.

Carberry NT 364697
The oldest part of the U-shaped mansion is the early sixteenth-century tower house forming the west wing. The south range is partly late sixteenth-century, and partly of the eight-

eenth and nineteenth centuries, while the east range is of 1860. Carberry went to Hugh Rigg in 1547 and then to the Dicksons, who sold it to the Duchess of Monmouth.

Catclune NT 351605
A ruined L-plan Sinclair house stood on the rocky outcrop.

Colinton NT 216694
The ruined sixteenth-century house of the Foulis family, with its blocked original entrance in a slight staircase projection, has a seventeenth-century kitchen wing.

Cousland NT 377681
There are traces of a sixteenth-century tower in woodland.

Craigcrook NT 211743
The Adamsons' sixteenth-century castle has a round corner tower, a square stair turret on the opposite side and later extensions. It is now used as an office block.

Craigmillar NT 285709 (AM)
Sir Simon Preston's L-plan tower of the 1370s stands above a low cliff and has on the other side a rectangular court of 1427 with a machicolated parapet and small round corner turrets. Here in 1477 James III is supposed to have done to death his brother John, Earl of Mar. In 1544 the castle was burnt by the English after they had removed valuables put in it for safety by the inhabitants of Edinburgh. The eastern domestic range was subsequently rebuilt and an outer court containing a chapel and dovecot was added.

After Rizzio's murder in Holyrood Palace in 1566 Queen Mary withdrew to quiet Craigmillar. There, with or without her connivance, the pact was made which resulted in the murder of her consort, Lord Darnley. The Prestons sold the castle in 1660 to Sir John Gilmour, President of the Court of Session, who rebuilt the western range as a residence.

Cramond NT 191769
A sixteenth-century tower with a round stair turret of a house of the Bishops of Dunkeld was restored in the 1970s.

Crichton NT 380612 (AM)
John de Crichton's tower house of about 1370 adjoins a hall block built by his son Sir William, Chancellor of Scotland in the 1440s. During the latter period the castle was assaulted by John Forrester of Corstorphine. The remainder of the buildings around a small court are of later in the fifteenth century. William, third Lord Crichton, was involved in the conspiracy of

the Duke of Albany against his brother James III and was besieged at Crichton by the royal forces in 1483, although he escaped to England.

The castle later went to the Hepburn Earls of Bothwell. On the forfeiture of the fourth Earl after his disastrous marriage to Queen Mary it was granted to Francis Stewart, created fifth Earl, who proved equally wild, and was finally forfeited in 1593. It was he who, after a period of exile in Europe, had an Italian architect remodel part of the courtyard with a fine Renaissance-type facade.

Dalhousie NT 320636

The Ramseys had a motte and bailey castle here, which they successfully defended against Henry IV in 1400. About 1450 they built a substantial L-plan tower surrounded by a court with its gateway flanked by an added round tower. Sir George Ramsey became a peer in 1618 and his son was created Earl of Dalhousie in 1633, the year which appears, along with his initials, on a new block connecting the tower with the west curtain, which has large windows in it. The work of transforming the castle into a gentlemanly seat continued in later centuries and it is now a hotel.

Dalkeith NT 333679

A small amount of masonry of a Douglas tower house and court survives in the walls of a mansion built in 1702-11 for the widowed Duchess of Monmouth and Buccleuch.

Edinburgh NT 252735

Although used from early times as a fortress, the earliest building on the volcanic crag is a small Norman chapel of the early twelfth century dedicated to Margaret, Malcolm Canmore's saintly queen. After Malcolm's death at Alnwick in 1093 the castle was besieged by his brother, Donald Bane, in support of his claim to the throne, and it was surrendered to the English in 1173, after King William's capture.

The castle had an English garrison from 1296 until 1313, when the Scots climbed the rock and surprised it. The defences were destroyed, but there was an English garrison there again for several years up to 1341, when William Douglas took it by a stratagem. In 1367-71 David II rebuilt the castle with lofty curtain walls and towers and in particular a mighty L-planned tower house, named after him.

After the murder of the young Earl of Douglas and his brother at the so called 'Black Dinner' of 1440 at the castle, it was captured after a nine-month siege by their relatives and required substantial repairs afterwards. James III's brother Alexander, Duke of Albany, escaped from imprisonment in David's Tower in 1479. James himself was confined in the tower by the nobles in 1482, but Alexander returned from exile, took his side and had him released. A new great hall was built in 1483 and other repairs were executed, but after James III's reign the castle ceased to be a royal residence except during minorities and crises. However, it remained of vital importance as the state armoury, prison, record repository and major fortress at the capital.

In 1566 Queen Mary gave birth to the future James VI in the castle. After her abdication it was held on her behalf against the Protestants until English help forced its surrender in 1573. Having been badly damaged by artillery, the castle was rebuilt to such an extent afterwards and in subsequent periods that all that survives of David II's defences is the lower half of his tower embedded within the Half Moon Battery.

The castle was captured in 1640 after a three-month siege by the Covenanters and Cromwell besieged it throughout the autumn of 1650. Much new work on the fortification was done by Charles II. The Jacobites failed to take it in both 1715 and 1745 and some of them were incarcerated in it later.

Hawthornden NT 287637

The castle stands on a sandstone rock which is hollowed out into caves beneath it. On the east or landward side of the triangular site is a ruined fifteenth-century tower with the gateway beside it. Only windows in the outer wall remain of a south range but there are inhabited apartments on the north which are the work of the poet Sir William Drummond and dated 1638, though much remodelled in later periods.

Hirendean NT 298512

On a hill is a fragment of a tower house of the Kers.

Holyroodhouse NT 169739 (AM)

James III found the guest range of Holyrood Abbey a comfortable alternative to the grim fortress of Edinburgh and James IV and James V developed what became the premier royal palace in Scotland. Much of their work was in timber and all that survived English destructions of 1544 and 1547 and rebuildings of the 1650s for Cromwell and the 1670s for Charles II was a tower house with round corner towers built in the 1530s to contain private apartments for James V. The palace of the 1670s has a wing matching this tower.

Inch NT 278709

This building stood on an island in a loch until about 1760. The south-west corner of the house is an L-plan tower, dated 1617 on a high stair turret in the re-entrant angle. A lower northern range is dated 1634 with the initials of John Winram. Inch was later held by the Gilmours.

Inveresk NT 348716
One wing of the mansion is a sixteenth-century tower.

Lauriston NT 204762 (P)
The south-west corner of the mansion is the tower built between 1587 and 1608 by Sir Archibald Napier. It bears the initials of his wife, Dame Elizabeth Mowbray, and was sold in 1683 to the Edinburgh goldsmith William Law.

Lennox NT 174671
Above the Water of Leith is the massive lower part of a fifteenth-century rectangular tower of the Lennox family.

Liberton NT 265697
The Dalmahoys' fifteenth-century tower stands on the hill.

Lochend NT 263743
The Logan's house and court on a rocky spur of Arthur's Seat are much rebuilt and extended.

Merchiston NT 243717
The Napiers built this substantial L-plan tower in the late fifteenth century, when several of them were successively the Chief Magistrate of Edinburgh. It is little altered externally and is chiefly associated with John Napier, the inventor of logarithms. It passed to the Scotts in 1699.

Newton NT 332699
A mansion of 1820 and 1835 contains seventeenth-century vaulted cellars and has nearby a sixteenth-century turret dovecot with gunports surviving from a barmkin.

Oxenfoord NT 388656
The Macgills' tower lies within the Adam mansion.

Pinkie NT 350727
The Abbot of Dunfermline's sixteenth-century tower was greatly extended by Alexander Seton, Earl of Dunfermline. After 1694 the Hays and Hopes made other additions.

Roseburn NT 226731
This mainly seventeenth-century building around a small court includes a tower with a round stair turret bearing the date 1582 and the arms and initials of Mungo Russell, Treasurer of Edinburgh, and his wife, Katherine Fisher.

Roslin NT 274628
The Sinclairs' castle on a spectacular site above the Esk was wrecked by Hertford in 1544. On the north side are remains of a fifteenth-century tower house and a wall with unusual rounded buttresses, while on the south side is a long range of apartments, now empty, with basements extending down the cliff. This part bears the dates 1597 and 1622 and the initials of Sir William Sinclair, his wife and son.

Sheriffhall NT 320680
The stair turret of the house now forms a dovecot.

Smeaton NT 347699
Parts of two round towers remain of a late courtyard castle incorporated into a house on the Dalkeith estate.

WEST LOTHIAN DISTRICT

Abercorn NT 083794
A mound in Hopetoun Park was excavated in 1963, revealing one wall of a medieval tower and remains of a manor house of the fifteenth to sixteenth centuries on the same site.

Barnbougle NT 169785
The existing building is mainly of 1881 but incorporates cellars from a ruin of the sixteenth and seventeenth centuries.

Blackness NT 056802
This fortress on a rocky shore looks rather like a ship. The enclosing walls, the block corresponding to the 'poop' and the tiny 'forecastle' are sixteenth-century work, but the 'main mast' is a tower house of about 1450 with a late seventeenth-century stair turret. Sir George Crichton's son, deprived of his inheritance, imprisoned his father here in the 1450s until the King besieged and captured the castle. It was later a prison and arsenal, retaining the latter function until the twentieth century. Monck captured the castle in 1654 from its hereditary captain, a Livingstone.

Bridge NS 944709
The early sixteenth-century L-plan tower of James Stewart and Helen Sinclair was extended by William, Earl of Linlithgow, after 1591. It was restored from ruin in the nineteenth century.

Cairns NT 091604
The Crichtons' ruined sixteenth-century castle has a wing flanking two sides of the main block.

Calder NT 073673

Lord Torphichen's L-plan mansion dated 1666 contains earlier and later work and has a gateway of 1670.

Carriber NS 966751

There are slight remains of Rob Gibb's tower of about 1540.

Carriden NT 026808

The L-plan tower, dated 1602, of Sir John Hamilton, Lord Bargany, passed to the Hopes, who extended and altered it.

Dundas NT 116767

The L-plan tower and a slightly later wing are datable by warrants issued in 1416 and 1424 to the Dundas family authorising work. The tower once housed a distillery but now lies empty beside a mansion. It retains its yett.

Duntarvie NT 091765

The Durhams' late sixteenth-century mansion is an unusually early symmetrical building with two corner towers at the back and the stair in the middle. Big windows face south.

Houston NT 058716

Sir Thomas Sharpe's tower house of about 1600 was extended in the eighteenth century, and again later for use as a hotel.

Kinneil NS 983804

At the beginning of his regency from 1542 to 1554 the Earl of Arran began the ruined block which forms the core of the house. To it, shortly before going into exile in France, he added the still roofed range on the north, which contains wall paintings. Ruined by the Earl of Morton, the house was not restored until 1677 for the Duchess of Hamilton.

Linlithgow NT 003774

The ruined royal palace stands on the site of a wooden pele built for Edward I in 1301-2. It was captured and destroyed in 1313. James I began the present building, erecting the massive eastern half containing the original entrance with the hall above. Work continued under James III and IV, and both James V and Mary were born in the palace, it being a frequent residence of queen consorts. James V added the present south entrance and part of the north range was remodelled for James VI in 1618. This work was finally finished for the visit of Charles I in 1633, the last time the palace was used by a king, though his son James, Duke of York, used it before succeeding to the throne in 1685. It was accidentally burnt out by Cumberland's troops in 1746.

117

Linnhouse NT 062630
The old part of the house has two square bodies touching each other at a corner and is dated 1589. An added wing has the initials of William Muirhead, who bought the house in 1631.

Lochcote NS 976737
A vaulted cellar survives north of Lochcote Reservoir.

Midhope NT 073787
The ruined tower house was formerly dated 1582 with the initials of Alexander Drummond and his wife. An extension of 1600 was heightened and a courtyard added by the Earl of Linlithgow in the seventeenth century.

Murieston NT 050636
A genuine tower house was made into a folly ruin in 1824.

Niddry NT 097743
The substantial L-plan tower house on a crag was built by George, fourth Lord Seton, killed at Flodden in 1513. Open battlements were later replaced by a further two storeys of rooms. Little remains of a barmkin.

Ochiltree NT 032748
The L-plan house bears the initials of Sir Archibald Stirling and Dame Grissel Ross and was dated 1610. It was remodelled later. Little remains of a court to the west.

Staneyhill NT 092784
This ruined seventeenth-century L-plan tower has decorated quoins and a chamfered stair turret in the re-entrant angle.

Orkney Islands

Birsay HY 248279
This ruined palace set around a courtyard is a purely domestic building constructed for Robert Stewart, Earl of Orkney, an illegitimate brother of Queen Mary. He and his son Patrick ruled Orkney in a semi-regal state, oppressing the people to fund their extravagances, until James VI had Patrick attainted for treason and executed in 1614.

Cairston HY 273096
The small ruined sixteenth-century enclosure with a tiny round turret at one corner is now a piggery. Excavations revealed another turret at the diagonally opposite corner.

Cobbie Row's HY 442264 (AM*)
The name is a corruption of Kolbein Hruga, the Norseman who built this small square tower, now reduced to its base, in 1145. There are extensions and an outer bank and ditch.

Kirkwall HY 450110 (AM)
The palace of Bishop Reid (1541-58) is a long ruined building with a substantial corner tower. It includes the lower part of a hall block of the twelfth or thirteenth century. In it Haakon IV died in 1263 after his ill-fated expedition to the Western Isles, and possibly also his grand-daughter Margaret, who expired when on her way to be crowned Queen of Scotland in 1290. The building was taken over by Patrick, Earl of Orkney, and about 1600 linked to a fine new palace, with notable oriels, which he built close by. The whole complex was returned to the bishops after a siege in 1614 and was occupied until Bishop Mackenzie's death in 1688.

Langskaill HY 434220
Two ranges, one habitable, one very ruined, lie on either side of a probably sixteenth-century court with its gateway flanked by gunports. The building bears the date 1676 and the initials of Sir William Craigie of Gairsay.

Noltland HY 430487 (AM*)
This massive Z-planned castle with two square wings and numerous gunports on the remote isle of Westray was built as a retreat for Gilbert Balfour, who had been involved in the murders of Cardinal Beaton in 1546 and Lord Darnley in 1567. Only foundations remain of a court and outbuildings.

Shetland Islands

Loch Strom HU 395475
On Castle Holm island are remains of a small tower.

Muness HP 629012
Laurence Bruce took up refuge in this remote spot under the protection of his half-brother Robert, Earl of Orkney, after a murder committed in an affray in his native Perthshire. His Z-planned castle of about 1590-1600 with two round towers is the most northerly castle in the British Isles.

Scalloway HU 405392
Patrick, Earl of Orkney's fine L-plan castle of about 1600, with the wing flanking two sides and with numerous stair turrets and bartizans, has been a ruin since about 1680.

Strathclyde Region
ARGYLL AND BUTE DISTRICT

Achadun NM 804392
   The Bishops of Lismore occupied this shattered thirteenth-century enclosure on Lismore until the sixteenth century.

Achallader NN 322442
   Only a fragment remains of Sir Duncan Campbell's small tower of about 1600 burnt by the Jacobites in 1689.

Airds NR 820383
   Traces of a Macdonald castle of enclosure granted to Sir Adam Reid in 1498 lie on the east side of Kintyre.

Am Fraoch Eilean NR 472627
   Traces of a castle lie on an islet off southern Jura.

Ardfad NM 769194
   On a rock on Seil are the foundations of a Z-plan castle and court built by the Macdougalls of Ardincaple about 1600.

Armaddy NM 785164
   Colin Campbell's mansion of 1737 incorporates the basement of a fifteenth-century tower of the Macdonalds of Rarey.

Aros NM 563450
   This thirteenth-century hall house and court overlooking the Sound of Mull were later a possession of the Macdonalds.

Ascog NR 946705
   Slight remains stand on the west side of Loch Ascog.

Barcaldine NM 907405
   Sir Duncan Campbell of Glenorchy's L-plan castle of 1601-9 has a round stair turret in the re-entrant angle. It was garrisoned in 1645 and 1678, but ruinous by about 1700. It was restored in 1897-1911 and re-covered with white harling.

Breachacha NM 159539
   This castle on Coll, restored from ruin in the 1970s, has a tower and a tiny court with a round tower. It basically dates from about 1430-50 though there are later alterations.

Cairnburgh NM 309440
   This castle has two completely separate enclosures on a pair of

islands in the Treshnish group. Each has traces of thin breastworks of a late date. It existed as early as 1249 and was usually a royal castle with local chiefs as keepers. James IV recovered it from the rebellious Lachlan Maclean in 1504, and later Macleans surrendered it to General Leslie in 1647, and to the Campbells in 1692.

Caisteal Nan Con NM 765136
On a rock off Torsa are foundations of a large tower and a court of the Macdougalls of Rarey, and later the Macleans.

Caisteal Na Nighinn Ruaidhe NM 916137
An island in Loch Avich bears the ruin of what is probably a thirteenth-century hall house of the Campbells.

Carnassery NM 837009
Though it looks like a tower house with a later extension, this building was entirely the work of John Carsewell, rector of Kilmartin and Bishop of the Isles in 1566-72. Of a court to the south there survives only a gateway dated 1681, with the initials of Sir Dougal Campbell and his wife.

Carrick NS 194944
On a rock near the mouth of Loch Goil is a fine ruined tower house of about 1400 with a tiny court facing the loch. Originally possibly a royal Stewart hunting seat, it was later held by the Murrays and was burnt by Argyll in 1685.

Castle Coeffin NM 853437
On a rock on Lismore is a ruined thirteenth-century hall house of the Macdougalls of Lorn, later held by the Campbells.

Castle Shuna NM 915482
The ruined tower was built by John Stewart (died 1595) or his son Duncan and was later given a round stair turret.

Castle Stalker NM 920473
On an islet is a tower house built about 1540 by Sir Alan Stewart as part of James V's scheme for keeping the peace in this area. In 1620 it was sold to Duncan Campbell, who added the existing battlements, but the Stewarts had it back, though only after a long siege, in 1685. A Stewart garrison finally surrendered to William III's forces in 1690. The tower was habitable until 1800 and was restored in the 1970s.

Castle Sween NR 712789
This quadrangular enclosure with a round-arched entrance, on the west side of Kintyre, probably dates from about 1200, when

this area was still under Norse rule. A tower house was added in the late thirteenth century and another tower in the sixteenth. It was held by the MacNeils of Gigha for the Macdonalds until 1481, when the Campbells became its keepers for the Crown. The castle was captured and dismantled by Alaisdair Colkitto Macdonald in 1645.

Duart NM 749354

After his marriage in 1366 Lachlan Maclean added a massive tower to a small square thirteenth-century castle of enclosure. His descendants made additions and alterations until their forfeiture in 1746, after which it became ruinous. The castle was restored in 1911-12.

Dun Ara NM 427577

A rock at the north end of Mull bears traces of a late enclosure of the Mackinnons with four structures within.

Dunaverty NR 688074

Only the last traces survive of this castle on a rock at the south end of Kintyre. It was recovered from rebels by the Crown in 1240, garrisoned against the Norsemen in 1263 and later held by the Macdonald Lords of the Isles. In 1494 James IV's governor was hanged from the walls by Sir John Macdonald within sight of the departing royal ship. The castle was damaged by Sussex in his raid on Kintyre in 1558. Archibald Macdonald's garrison was massacred after submitting to General Leslie in 1647. The castle was finally dismantled during Argyll's rebellion of 1685.

Dunollie NM 852314

A headland north of Oban bears a small square ruined court with a tower house at one corner, built by John Macdougall after 1451. It was captured by Argyll in 1644-5.

Dunoon NS 175764

On a hillock are fragments of a small enclosure.

Dunstaffnage NM 882344 (AM)

An enclosure of about 1270, with two rounded towers and a gatehouse, is crammed on a knob of conglomerate by the mouth of Loch Etive. Built by the Macdougalls of Lorn, it was captured by Bruce in 1309. It was later held by the Stewarts and then from about 1470 by the Campbells, who converted the gatehouse into a tower house. The castle was burnt by Argyll in 1685 and had a government garrison in 1715 and 1745. The gatehouse was gutted by fire in 1810 but repaired about a century later. The remainder is ruinous.

Duntrune NR 794956
A promontory by Loch Crinan bears a tiny thirteenth-century enclosure with a seventeenth-century L-plan house and other internal buildings. Argyll burnt it in 1685.

Dunyveg NR 406455
Only very scanty remains survive of this castle on Islay.

Finchurn NM 898044
On a rock near the south end of Loch Awe is a ruined hall house built by the Macdougalls in the thirteenth century.

Fraoch Eilean NN 108251
This ruined hall house on an island in Loch Awe was in 1267 granted to Gillechrist MacNaughton by Alexander III. Later the Campbells built a house within part of it.

Gylem NM 805265
Duncan Macdougall's small but fine L-plan tower was completed in 1582. Access between small inner and outer courts was through part of the basement and was protected by machicolations in an oriel at the top. The castle was captured and burnt by General Leslie's forces in 1647.

Innischonnel NM 976119
This impressive thirteenth-century square court on an island in Loch Awe was the original chief seat of the Campbells until they transferred to Inveraray. There are alterations and two outer courts of the fifteenth century. John Macdougall held it against Bruce in 1308. The castle was later a prison and was abandoned about 1704.

Island Muller NR 756224
On the east side of the Kintyre peninsula on a rock is the base of a fifteenth-century Macdonald tower.

Kames NS 064676
The Bannatynes' tower of uncertain date on Bute has a late sixteenth-century wing and restored battlements.

Kilchurn NN 133276 (AM)
About 1440 Sir Colin Campbell of Glenorchy built a tower and barmkin on an island, now a promontory, at the north end of Loch Awe. Later additions were a hall and the four bartizans on the tower, and in 1614 Sir Duncan Campbell rebuilt the south-west range. The Campbells withstood a two-day siege in 1654 by General Middleton before he retreated before Monck's forces. After the war of 1685 John Campbell, Earl of Breadal-

bane, provided the barmkin with three round flanking towers and extensive barrack room accommodation on the west side. However, he rarely resided at Kilchurn, nor would he allow the government to use it as a garrison post until 1715. Repairs to the ruin are proceeding in the 1980s.

Kilkerran NR 729194
James IV erected a castle here about 1498 but the small fragment in a garden is of rather later date.

Kilmartin NR 836991
The late sixteenth-century ruined manse is Z-planned with two round corner towers and an extra round stair turret.

Lachlan NS 006954
The Maclachlans' fifteenth-century castle, occupied until 1746, lies on a rock by Loch Fyne. It comprises a pair of tenement blocks separated only by a very narrow court.

Loch Finlaggan NR 388681
Only slight remains survive on an island on an Islay loch.

Meikle Kilmory NS 051611
On a crag by a farm is the base of a small square tower of about 1600 with an added round corner turret.

Moy NM 616247
Hector Maclean's fifteenth-century tower later had its upper parts remodelled. It was involved in the Maclean-Campbell struggle of the 1670s and was abandoned about 1752.

Rothesay NS 086646
This Stewart castle is first mentioned in 1230 when the Norsemen captured it by breaching the late twelfth-century wall with their axes. A gate tower had been added about 1220 and four round towers were added after the Norse invasion of 1263. Robert II and Robert III favoured Rothesay as a residence; they probably added the chapel and possibly began the extension of the gatehouse into a tower house, though most of the latter is the work of James IV and V in about 1512 and 1541. The castle was besieged by the Earl of Ross about 1462, by the Master of Ruthven in 1527, and by the Earl of Lennox in 1544. It was not reoccupied after being burnt by Argyll in 1685, although the Marquis of Bute made repairs in 1900.

Saddell NR 789315
The tower and barmkin were built about 1508-12 by David Hamilton, Bishop of Argyll, to replace Achadun on Lismore. It

was burned by Sussex in 1558 and was later held by the Macdonalds and then the Campbells. The existing outbuildings are mostly of 1770, much of the barmkin wall and buildings of nearby Saddell Abbey being destroyed to provide materials. The tower is now restored and in use as a holiday home.

Skipness NR 907577
The Macdonalds' early thirteenth-century hall house and chapel were in about 1300 incorporated into opposite end walls of a courtyard. After 1493 it went to the Campbells, who built up a tower house in one corner. They successfully held the castle against Colkitto Macdonald in the 1640s.

Tarbert NR 867687
On a hill dominating the Tarbert isthmus on Kintyre are foundations of a royal thirteenth-century courtyard castle. Bruce added a large outer bailey with at least four towers about 1315-25, and James IV added the ruined tower house on the south side. Walter Campbell of Skipness captured it from its hereditary keeper, the Earl of Argyll, in 1685.

Toward NS 119678
The now restored seat of the Lamonts consists of a fifteenth-century tower and a sixteenth-century court with a decorated gateway. The Campbells captured the Royalist Lamont castle of Toward, and Ascog opposite on Bute, in 1646, massacring or otherwise badly treating those within.

Wester Kames NS 062681
This small square tower of about 1600 with a round stair turret was restored in 1905 by the Marquis of Bute.

CLYDESDALE AND GLASGOW AREA
(VARIOUS DISTRICTS)

Auchinvole NS 714769
The mansion incorporated a sixteenth-century tower house.

Avondale NS 701447
The ruined tower of Andrew Stewart, made Lord Avondale in 1457, stands on a mound with fragments of a barmkin wall. A square wing and a round tower were added in the sixteenth century and it was occupied by the Hamiltons up to 1717.

Bardowie NS 580739
The tower house is dated 1566 with the initials of the Hamiltons, owners until the mid eighteenth century. There are alterations and extensions of about 1700 and later.

Bedlay NS 692700

Robert, Lord Boyd's late sixteenth-century house, with a square stair turret flanking two sides, was extended in the seventeenth century by James Robertson, Lord Bedlay, the new work having two round turrets and a square one.

Boghall NT 041370

Only three fragments remain of the late sixteenth-century seat of the Fleming Earls of Wigtown, with a large hexagonal court with a gatehouse, three round towers with gunports, and a T-shaped house on the south-east.

Bothwell NS 688594

Walter de Moravia's castle by the Clyde was designed about 1260 as a great pentagonal enclosure with a massive round keep at one corner, round towers at three other corners, and a twin-towered gatehouse at the fifth. However, only the keep and parts of the adjacent walls were completed before the Wars of Independence. The castle suffered a fourteen-month siege by the Scots in 1298-9 and a siege of a month in 1301, when Edward I recovered it and installed Aymer de Valance as his Warden of Scotland. It was surrendered and destroyed after the English defeat at Bannockburn, half of the keep being tumbled by the Scots into the Clyde.

Edward III had the castle roughly patched up in 1336 but it was captured and dismantled again in 1337. It lay waste until 1362 when it was taken over by Archibald the Grim, Lord of Galloway. He made Bothwell his principal seat, creating a rectangular court half the size of the planned original. His son added the hall and adjacent round and square towers. The castle was later held by the Crichtons, Ramseys, Hepburns and Douglases, and in the late seventeenth century it was dismantled for its materials.

Cadzow NS 734537

This Hamilton castle, dramatically positioned on a cliff above the Avon Water, was similar to Craignethan Castle.

Castlemilk NS 608594

A tower probably of the late fifteenth century adjoins a later Stewart mansion now used for institutional purposes.

Cathcart NS 586599

This ruin was demolished to its base by Glasgow City Council about 1979. Built about 1450 by the Cathcarts, it passed in 1546 to the Semphills, who occupied it until 1740. A tower with a thick end wall containing mural chambers was surrounded by a rectangular court with round corner turrets.

Colzium NS 729788

Incorporated in the garden wall of the house is part of a Livingstone tower once dated 1575 and destroyed in 1703.

Corehouse NS 882414

Above the Corra Linn falls on the Clyde is the ruined castle of the Bannatynes, with apartments on one side of a small court. It was sold in 1695 to William Somerville.

Couthally NS 972482

There are only slight remains of the sixteenth-century L-plan tower and courtyard which formed the chief seat of the Somervilles before they removed to Drum in Midlothian.

Covington NS 975399

The Lindseys' massive, now ruined fifteenth-century tower was sold to Sir George Lockhart in the seventeenth century.

Craignethan NS 816464 (AM)

The castle built in the 1530s by Sir James Hamilton of Finnart stands on a promontory above the Nethan and has a low residential tower house surrounded by a rectangular court with corner and mid-wall towers and a thick and high rampart shielding the one weak side, where there was an outer court. Clearance of the ditch in front has revealed an almost complete caponier flanking its bottom. The castle is thus designed for defence against and by artillery. It was later held by the Earl of Arran, Regent for the young Queen Mary for twelve years. He opposed her marriage to Darnley but in 1567 he led her forces against the Regent Moray. After defeat at Langside in 1568 the Hamiltons surrendered Craignethan and Cadzow but recaptured them under Arran's son Lord Claude in 1569. The two castles were finally taken over by the Protestants after the Hamiltons fled to exile in 1579 and at both the defences of the inner court were slighted. Craignethan remained in use, however, and in 1659 Andrew Hay built a new house in the outer court which is still inhabited. The rest is ruinous.

Crawford NS 954214

A motte by the Clyde bears ruins of apartment blocks and a small court built by the Lindsay Earls of Crawford.

Crookston NS 524628

The remarkable ruined tower house of about 1400 of the Stewarts of Darnley is ashlar-faced with rib vaults and corner turrets.

Crossbasket NS 666559

This sixteenth-century jointure house of the Lindsays of Mains is much altered and incorporated into a later mansion.

Dalzell NS 756550
A fifteenth-century tower stands in the middle of one side of a rectangular sixteenth-century court with one round corner tower. Apartments on the east and south sides are dated 1649 with the initials of James Hamilton, who bought the castle from Lord Dalziell. Much work was done in 1857.

Douglas NS 843318
The castle of the Douglases was destroyed by James II in 1455 and replaced by a tower, which in the late seventeenth century was itself replaced by a mansion. This was destroyed in 1755 by a fire and a fragment of a corner tower and some cellars of outbuildings are all that remains.

Garrion NS 797512
Incorporated into the mansion is a small tower with a stair wing probably built for James Hamilton about 1605.

Gilbertfield NS 653588
This lofty ruined house with a long wing is dated 1607.

Haggs NS 560626 (P)
The restored L-plan building with bartizans and prolific cable mouldings has the year 1585 and the names of Sir John Maxwell and Dame Margaret Conyngham on it and is now a museum.

Hallbar NS 839471
This empty tiny square tower house and its now destroyed barmkin on a promontory were granted to Harie Stewart in 1581 and acquired by Sir George Lockhart of Lee about 1662.

Jerviston NS 760581
This small L-plan tower of about 1600 with altered roofs bears the initials RB and EH above the entrance.

Jerviswood NS 884455
The Baillies' mid seventeenth-century house adjoins the last remains of the Livingstones' sixteenth-century tower.

Mains NS 627560
The Lindsays' fifteenth-century tower near a motte was sold about 1695, unroofed in 1723 and restored in the 1970s.

Monkland NS 730633
The house has a long main block with a square tower facing the approach and two round towers on the other side.

Pollok NS 522570
The mansion, dated 1686 and 1687 with the initials of Sir Robert Pollok and Annabel Maxwell, incorporates part of a tower of about 1500 and was restored after a fire in 1882.

Stonebyres NS 838433
The de Veres' fifteenth-century tower was doubled in length and given bartizans and dormer windows in the sixteenth century. It was encased in a mansion in the nineteenth century.

The Peel NS 594561
The nucleus of the house is a sixteenth-century tower.

Torrance NS 654526
A sixteenth-century L-plan tower has had a stair turret added in the re-entrant angle and other additions made.

Waygateshaw NS 825484
The old house, with a roll-moulded courtyard gateway flanked by gunports, is being restored in the 1980s.

Woodhead NS 606783
High above the Glazert Water is a tower built in the 1570s for John Lennox of Balcorrach. It was left as a picturesque ruin when Lennox Castle was built nearby about 1840.

CUNNINGHAME AND KILMARNOCK DISTRICTS

Aiket NS 388488
Alexander Cunninghame's tower of about 1479 was extended, probably by a descendant of the same name who was shot near the castle shortly after being an accessory to the murder of the Earl of Eglinton in 1586. The castle was later remodelled as a house but restoration in the early 1980s has given it a late sixteenth-century aspect again.

Ardrossan NS 233424
The Ardrossans' small square courtyard castle of the thirteenth century on a strong site was remodelled by the Montgomeries in the fourteenth to sixteenth centuries, the gatehouse becoming a tower house. It is now very ruinous.

Auchans NS 355346
The Wallaces' early seventeenth-century house with a stair turret in the middle of one side was converted by Sir William Cochrane into an L-plan mansion formerly dated 1644. It passed to the Earls of Eglinton and became a ruin.

Auchenharvie NS 363443

Amid quarry pits is a ruinous Cunninghame tower of about 1500.

Barr NS 502365

In the middle of Galston is an early sixteenth-century tower of the Lockharts now used as a meeting place.

Blair NS 305480

The fifteenth-century tower and a southern extension were remodelled as a gabled mansion and given a stair turret with the date 1617 and the initials of Bryce Blair and Annabel Wallace. A western wing bears the date 1668 and the initials of William Blair and Lady Margaret Hamilton.

Brodick NR 016378 (NT)

The Stewarts had a castle here which was attacked by Bruce's forces in 1307. It was destroyed by an English fleet in 1406 and by the Lord of the Isles about 1455. The first Hamilton Earl of Arran built a tower house about 1510 which was damaged in a raid on Arran by the sons of Ninian Stewart in 1528. It was damaged again in 1544 by the Lennox Stewarts and was lengthened and remodelled by the Regent Arran after he retired from public life in the late 1550s. Brodick was seized by the Campbells in 1639; although recovered by the Duke of Hamilton, in 1646 another Campbell garrison was installed in the castle and under siege by the islanders. Later the castle was occupied by a Cromwellian garrison and a battery was added on the east. This contained the entrance until extensive additions were made in 1844.

Caprington NS 407363

The Wallaces' massive early tower, a tiny stair wing, a substantial later wing and the rock on which they stood were encased by Sir William Cunningham's work of about 1800.

Cessnock NS 511355

This strongly sited mansion set around a court bears the dates 1666 outside and 1680 inside, referring to Sir Hew Campbell. It includes Sir George Campbell's late sixteenth-century work and John Campbell's tower house of the 1520s. It was restored by the Duke of Portland in the nineteenth century.

Clonbeith NS 338455

In a farmyard is the basement of a Cunninghame house dated 1607. It was sold to the Earl of Eglinton in 1717.

Corsehill NS 416456

Near Stewarton is a fragment of an early Cunninghame tower.

Crawfurdland NS 456408
The Crawfurds' tower of about 1550 adjoins a large mansion.

Crosbie NS 217500
This Crawford house is a purely domestic T-planned building of the seventeenth century, now in a caravan park.

Dean NS 437394 (P)
About 1460 the Boyds added a courtyard and a hall block to a massive tower house of about 1360. From 1466 to 1469 they had possession of the young James III and ruled Scotland in his name. On their downfall Sir Alexander Boyd was executed for treason while his brother Lord Boyd and nephew the Earl of Arran fled to Denmark. James Boyd added a porch to the hall block about 1650. His son William was created Earl of Kilmarnock in 1661, a title lost with the forfeiture of William, fourth Earl, after the 1745 Jacobite rebellion. The ruined castle was restored by Lord Howard de Walden in the 1930s and the Dean now serves Kilmarnock as a museum and park.

Dundonald NS 364345 (AM*)
Dundonald was a favoured residence of Robert II and his son Robert III. The former built a large tower house, with a rib-vaulted great hall on its top storey, on the remains of the gatehouse of a thirteenth-century courtyard castle. Dundonald was later held by the Boyds and Wallaces.

Fairlie NS 213549
Beside the Fairlie Glen is the ruined tower built about 1500 by the Fairlies and sold to the Boyles in 1650.

Giffen NS 377507
Most of this fifteenth-century Montgomery tower house collapsed in 1838. Only traces remain in a garden by a cliff.

Glengarnock NS 311574
On a promontory above the Garnock Burn is a fourteenth-century Cunninghame tower with a fifteenth-century block set in front of the one approachable side. The latter became part of a court in the sixteenth century, when also the vaulted kitchen, now the only complete room, was built.

Hessilhead NS 379533
There are scanty traces of a Montgomery tower hidden away in shrubs. It was extended about 1685 and dismantled in 1776.

Hunterston NS 193515
The Hunters' early sixteenth-century tower has a seventeenth-century extension with a square stair turret.

Kelburn NS 217567 (P, grounds only)

A Z-plan castle of about 1590-1600, with two round towers and the initials of John Boyle and Marion Crawford, adjoins the 1722 mansion of David Boyle, first Earl of Glasgow.

Kerelaw NS 269428

Fragments of a sixteenth-century Cunninghame courtyard mansion lie beside a stream north of Stevenston.

Kilbirnie NS 304541

Malcolm Crawfurd's tower of about 1480 and John Crawfurd's mansion of about 1627 are ruins touching at a single corner.

Kildonan NR 037210

This small ruined tower in a garden at the south end of Arran existed by 1406 when granted to John of Ardgowan.

Knock NS 194631

Near Robert Steel's mansion of 1850 is a derelict Z-plan castle with two round turrets bearing the date 1604 and the initials of one of the Frasers and IB, his wife.

Law NS 211484

This ruined tower on Law Hill is supposed to have been built for James III's sister Mary on her marriage to Thomas Boyd in 1468. Major Hugh Bontin obtained it from William Boyd, Earl of Kilmarnock, in 1670. A restoration is planned.

Little Cumbrae NS 153514

Hew, Earl of Eglinton, built this ruined tower on an islet in about 1515-20 to protect Cumbrae from piratical raids. A contract of 1568 concerns the provison of glass windows (rare until about that time) at the Earl's residences of Ardrossan, Irvine, Eglinton, Polnoon, Glasgow and Cumbrae.

Loch Ranza NR 933507 (AM*)

This ruined hall house on Arran was probably built for John of Menteith, created Lord of Knapdale and Arran in 1315. It was granted to Alexander Montgomerie, Lord Skelmorlie, in 1452 and about a century later was drastically remodelled.

Loudon NS 506378

The Crawfurds' tower of about 1480-1500 and the mansion of John Campbell, Chancellor of Scotland, created Earl of Loudon in 1633, are encased in a large mansion of 1807, which became a ruin after 1945. It surrendered to Cromwell's forces in 1650.

Monk NS 292474

This T-plan ruin with thin walls was built in the early

seventeenth century for the Hamilton Earl of Abercorn.

Montfode NS 226441
Only one round turret remains of a Montgomerie Z-plan castle of about 1600.

Newmilns NS 536374
The mid sixteenth-century tower of the Campbells in the middle of the town was used as a prison for Covenanters in the seventeenth century and now lies in the backyard of a pub.

Portincross NS 176488
This tower on a rock by the shore has a wing projecting from an end wall. Robert II and Robert III are said to have used it as an embarkation point for trips to Rothesay. It was held by the Boyds until 1737, though only used by fishermen from the 1660s. The roof was blown off in 1739.

Rowallan NS 435424 (AM)
Gilchrist Muir was given Rowallan as a reward for useful service at the battle of Largs in 1263. A much damaged early tower may be his work. The south range with the principal apartments was built for Mungo Muir, killed at Pinkie in 1547, while the east range, with a twin-turreted gateway with cable mouldings, and the back wall of the tiny court are the work of his son John and are dated 1562 (or 1567). The building in the north-west corner is an addition of the 1640s, with the initials of Sir William Muir and Dame Jane Hamilton, while the gateway of an outer court is dated 1661, with the initials of his son, another William, and Dame Elizabeth Hamilton. The most famous of all the Muirs was Elizabeth, wife of Robert II and mother of Robert III. The castle was later held by the Earl of Loudon and now lies empty.

Skelmorlie NS 195658
The Montgomeries' tower house of 1502 and one round tower of its barmkin are incorporated in John Graham's mansion of about 1850. The upper parts of the tower house are of about 1600.

Stane NS 338399
A small Montgomerie tower of the early sixteenth century was remodelled as a folly about 1750 and is now ruinous.

Treesbank NS 420346
The Campbells' house of 1672, enlarged in 1838, has as its nucleus a sixteenth-century tower house.

Bannachra NS 343843
The ruined Colquhoun castle lies in a garden. It or a predecessor was attacked in 1592 by the Macgregors.

Darleith NS 345806
A mansion incorporates the Darleiths' tower house.

Dumbarton NS 400745 (AM, permanently closed)
The rock bore a royal fortress from early times but the existing defences are of the late seventeenth century and 1790, except for the fourteenth-century Portcullis Arch. Patrick Galbraith seized the castle during the civil wars of the 1440s, and in 1498 James IV captured it from Lord Darnley. Both James IV and James V used it as a base for naval expeditions to the west coast. The castle was captured in 1545 by Regent Arran from the Earl of Lennox, and in 1571 John Hamilton, Archbishop of St Andrews, was executed after it, and he, fell to the Protestants. It changed hands several times during the Covenant wars and was surrendered in 1652 to Cromwell's forces. A party of Royalists raided the castle in 1654. It remained in military use until 1945.

Dunglass NS 435735
On a headland behind an oil refinery are remains of a house and courtyard of the Colquhouns, dating from the fifteenth and sixteenth centuries. They were dismantled in the eighteenth century.

Kilmahew NS 352787
By a mansion is the late ruined castle of the Napiers.

Loch Lomond NS 369904, 373863, 323096, 332128
Little remains of the four island castles of Inch Galbraith, Inchmurrin, Inveruglas and Vow.

Mains NS 446877
The Dennistouns' lofty fifteenth-century tower was later held by the Cunninghame Earl of Glencairn and by the Cochranes.

Rosneath NS 272823
The Marquis of Argyll's house of about 1630 at the south-east end of the bay was not restored after a fire in 1802.

Rossdhu NS 361896
Most of the late tower of the Colquhouns of Luss was demolished in 1770 to provide materials for a new mansion.

KYLE AND CARRICK AND CUMNOCK AND DOON VALLEY DISTRICTS

Ailsa Craig NX 023995
On one side of this spectacular 1100 foot (335 m) high rock in the Clyde estuary is a small ruined sixteenth-century tower.

Ardmillan NX 169945
This much altered Kennedy castle, burnt out in the twentieth century, orginally had a block with two round turrets facing a small court. About 1680, after recently passing to the Crawfurds, it was described as strongly built, moated and 'able to secure the owner from the suddain commotions and assaults of the wild people of this corner, which upon these occasions are set upon robbery and depredation...'.

Ardstinchar NX 086824
Only a ruined tower and various fragments remain of Hugh Kennedy's courtyard castle of about 1440-60 with several towers on a rocky hilltop site. In 1601 Gilbert Kennedy, baron of Bargany and Ardstinchar, was killed in an unequal fight near Maybole against his kinsman and rival the Earl of Cassillis.

Auchencloigh NS 495166
Slight traces of a sixteenth-century tower remain by a farm.

Auchinleck NS 500232
Little remains of the Boswells' L-plan castle of about 1620.

Ayr NS 333223
Nothing remains of a thirteenth-century courtyard castle and only a fragment remains of a pentagonal fort of the 1650s.

Baltersan NS 282087
This fine ruined L-plan tower with an oriel at the top of the wing was built about 1580 for David Kennedy of Penyglen.

Brounston NS 261012
The Kennedy T-plan castle of about 1620 is now very ruinous.

Carleton NX 143895
By a farm is the ruined sixteenth-century Cathcart tower.

Cassillis NS 511355
Sir John Kennedy's massive tower of about 1370 was remodelled and given a stair wing in the early seventeenth century by his descendant the Earl of Cassillis. There are

extensions of 1832. Culzean was the family seat from the 1770s till the 1940s but the Marquis of Ailsa is now back at Cassillis.

Cloncaird NS 359075
Henry Richie's mansion of 1814 incorporates the much altered sixteenth-century tower house of Walter Mure.

Craigie NS 408317
The Lindsays' ruined hall house of about 1230-40 was remodelled in the fifteenth century as a tower house by the Wallaces and given a courtyard and outbuildings on each side.

Craigneil NX 147854
This ruined fifteenth-century tower on a hill now stands directly above the edge of a quarry pit.

Crossraguel NS 275084
Beside the abbot's lodging of the abbey is a ruined square tower house added about 1530 by Abbot William Kennedy.

Culzean NS 233103
Robert Adam's masterpiece, created in the 1770s for the ninth and tenth Earls of Cassillis, incorporates part of Sir Thomas Kennedy's late sixteenth-century L-plan tower.

Dalblair (or Kyle) NS 647192
On a promontory is a fragment of Cunninghame tower.

Dalquharran NS 273019
A palace house of about 1490-1500 with a square stair wing and a round tower has an even more ruined wing. On the stair turret between the two is the date 1679, and on a fireplace are the initials of Sir James and Dame Margaret Kennedy.

Dinvin and Dalmellington NS 201932 and 482058
These two impressive Norman castle mounds are the finest of quite a number of mottes in what used to be Ayrshire.

Dunaskin (or Burnhead) NS 450089
A promontory above the Dunaskin Burn is cut off by a ditch and bears the foundations of a large early tower.

Dunduff NS 272164
Overlooking the sea are remains of a Kennedy L-plan castle of about 1600 with a stair turret in the re-entrant angle.

Dunure NS 253158
An early Kennedy tower house on this rock by the sea was

extended and rebuilt in the fifteenth century to form the main building, while in the late sixteenth century a long range was added on the landward side providing kitchens. In the 1550s Gilbert Kennedy, Earl of Cassillis, obtained the lands of Glenluce Abbey by very dubious means and then attempted to do likewise with those of Crossraguel. He had Allan Stewart, the lay abbot, tortured at Dunure in an attempt to make him sign away the lands. Hearing of this, Kennedy of Bargany stormed the castle one morning, and, after Earl Gilbert had failed to retake it, removed Stewart to Ayr, where a compromise agreeable to all was worked out.

Greenan NS 312193
This tower and a tiny barmkin on a cliff formerly bore the date 1603 and the initials of John Kennedy of Baltersan.

Kiers NS 430081
Only traces remain of a thirteenth-century courtyard castle.

Kilkenzie NS 308082
John Baird's late sixteenth-century tower was restored and incorporated into a mansion in the nineteenth century.

Kilkerran NS 293005
Only half of a Fergusson tower of about 1500 remains standing, high above a stream.

Killochan NS 227004
This lofty L-plan castle, with a round tower on the outer corner and a square turret in the re-entrant angle, bears the date 1586 and the name 'Ihone Cathcart of Carltoun'.

Kingenclough NS 503256
The Campbells' L-plan house of about 1600 is very ruinous.

Kirkhill NX 146859
Beside a mansion at Colmonell is an L-plan ruin dated 1589 with the initials of Thomas and Janet Kennedy.

Knockdolian NX 123854
A now ruined Graham tower of about 1500 was rebuilt in about 1600-40.

Loch Doon NX 483950 (AM*)
This ruined ashlar-faced thirteenth-century polygonal court-yard castle with traces of internal buildings, including a sixteenth-century tower house, was rebuilt on the shore of the loch after the water level was raised to supply Ayr. Built

probably by the Bruce Earls of Carrick, the castle was captured by the English in 1306, while in 1333 it was one of the six strongholds which held out for David II against the usurper Edward Balliol. In 1510 it was captured from the Kennedys by William Crawfurd of Lochmores.

Martnaham NS 395173
On a promontory jutting far into the loch is the lower part of a thinly walled building, probably of late date.

Mauchline NS 496273
The prior of a cell of Melrose Abbey lived in the tower of about 1500, lying by a stream in the town. In a still inhabited later extension to the south Robert Burns was married.

Maybole NS 301100
The fine L-plan tower with an oriel window on the caphouse of the stair wing was built about 1620-30 by John, sixth Earl of Cassillis, a leading statesman of his day.

Newark NS 324173
This jointure house of the Kennedys of Bargany has a tower of about 1500 and a later extension on a rock, and some more recent buildings at a lower level. In 1602 the laird of Auchindrayne took refuge with Duncan Crawfurd here after the murder of Sir Thomas Kennedy of Culzean, to which he was regarded as an accomplice.

Penkill NS 232985
Spencer Boyd in 1857 restored a small tower of about 1600, to which Thomas Boyd had added in 1628 a long range.

Pinwherry NX 198867
Johnnie Kennedy's ruined L-plan tower of about 1590 has a square stair turret corbelled out above the re-entrant angle like that at Baltersan. It was later held by the Earl of Carrick.

Sorn NS 548269
The Hamiltons built a modest tower in the early sixteenth century and then created a range by extending it. It passed to the Seton Earl of Winton in 1585 and in the early seventeenth century was sold to the Earl of Loudon.

Sundrum NS 410213
Lord Hamilton's house of 1793, now a hotel, incorporates Sir Duncan Wallace's much altered tower of the 1370s.

Terringzean NS 556205
An ashlar-faced ruined tower and wall of about 1400 adjoin

traces of a thirteenth-century hall house overlain by a smaller, later building. The court is protected by a ditch.

Thomaston NS 240096
Thomas Corr's early sixteenth-century castle has the entrance to a former courtyard in the base of the wing. It passed to the M'Ilvanes of Grimmet and was used until about 1800.

Trabboch NS 448222
There are slight remains of a fifteenth-century tower.

Turnberry NS 196073
Around the lighthouse are the last traces of the inner and outer courts of a thirteenth-century castle of the Earls of Carrick. Bruce had the castle, then his own property, dismantled about 1310, and it was probably not restored.

RENFREW, EASTWOOD AND INVERCLYDE DISTRICTS

Barcraig NS 397565
A small part of a sixteenth-century tower lies by the B776.

Barochan NS 415686
The Flemings' much altered sixteenth-century tower is incorporated into a nineteenth-century mansion.

Barr NS 347582
A ruined tower and a small court were built in the early sixteenth century although the former bears the dates 1680 and 1699 with initials of two of the Ferguslie Hamiltons.

Blackhall NS 490630
Stewart of Ardgowan's house of about 1600 was restored in 1983.

Dargavel NS 433693
Adjoining a mansion is a Z-plan castle with round turrets bearing the date 1584 with Maxwell arms and initials.

Duchal NS 334685
On a strong promontory site are ruins of an early tower and enclosure, possibly of the thirteenth century. It was a possession of the Lyles, peers from 1446, and passed in 1544 to the Porterfield family, becoming ruinous soon afterwards.

Elliston NS 392598
In a garden are remains of an early sixteenth-century tower house and courtyard.

Houston NS 412672

Most of the courtyard house of the Stewart Earls of Lennox was pulled down in 1780, leaving only one range dated 1625 though including both earlier and later work in it.

Inverkip NS 205728

On a cliff in the grounds of the present mansion is a ruined Stewart tower house of about 1500. A later wing has gone.

Leven NS 216764

The Mortons' tower of about 1500 was before completion given a wing just touching it at one corner. It passed to the Sempills in 1547 and later to the Schaw Stewarts. Now lying by a new housing estate, it is to be restored in the 1980s.

Mearns NS 553553

Beside a church of 1971 on a crag, and serving it with rooms, is Herbert, Lord Maxwell's tower licensed in 1449. It passed to the Stewarts in the late seventeenth century.

Newark NS 331745 (AM)

Patrick Maxwell's large mansion, bearing the dates 1597 and 1599, now stands among the shipyards of Port Glasgow. It incorporates a small tower and a barmkin gatehouse of about 1490. Patrick was involved in various local feuds and murders in the late sixteenth century, yet he became a justice of the peace in 1623. James IV was the guest of George Maxwell here in 1495.

Old Bishopton NS 422717

The Brisbanes' much altered and extended seventeenth-century L-plan house was later held by the Walkinshaws, the Dunlops, the Sempills and finally the Maxwells of Pollok.

Polnoon NS 586513

On a motte above the Dunwan Burn are fragments of Sir John Montgomery's tower house of about 1388.

Ranforlie NS 384652

The Knox family's small ruined sixteenth-century tower and court lie in bushes by a golf course. It was later held by William Cochrane, Earl of Dundonald, and the Aikenheads.

Stanely NS 464616

In the reservoir is the early sixteenth-century L-plan tower of the Maxwells. It was sold to Lady Ross in 1629 and was later held by the Boyle Earls of Glasgow.

Tayside Region
ANGUS AND DUNDEE CITY DISTRICTS

Affleck NO 493389
The Afflecks' fine L-plan tower of about 1480 with an oratory in the upper part of the stair wing was held by the Reids from the mid seventeenth century until forfeiture in 1776.

Airlie NO 293522
Of the castle of enclosure which Sir James Ogilvie was licensed to build in 1432 only the strong front curtain and the entrance remain, the domestic quarters having been rebuilt after a siege and demolition in 1640 by Argyll.

Ardestie NO 505342
Stones of the Earl of Panmure's castle with the dates 1625 and 1688 are reset on a farmhouse and a cottage.

Auchterhouse NO 332373
The much rebuilt mansion has sixteenth-century work of the Earls of Buchan and seventeenth-century work of the Earl of Strathmore. It was later held by the Ogilvie Earls of Airlie. In the garden is the basement of a massive early tower house.

Auchtermeggities NO 553497
Reset in the gateposts and a garage of the mansion of Balmadies are shotholes and panels dated 1615 and 1657.

Balfour NO 337546
Attached to a farmhouse is a lofty round tower remaining from Walter Ogilvie's mid sixteenth-century castle.

Balgavies NO 542513
Near the modern mansion is a fragment of a Lindsay castle destroyed by James VI in 1594 after the Catholic rebellion.

Ballinshoe NO 417532
The ruined Lindsay tower of about 1600 has a bartizan which was originally balanced at the opposite corner by a turret.

Ballumbie NO 445344
Parts of a Lovel courtyard castle of the fifteenth or sixteenth century, including two round towers, are incorporated into the derelict stableyard of the equally derelict modern mansion.

Balmossie NO 476326
Parts of a sixteenth-century castle are reset in a mill.

Balnamoon NO 552638
The north-west wing of the mansion of about 1820-30 is the Collaces' tower of about 1490, later held by the Carnegies.

Bonnyton NO 661557
Only two reset heraldic panels survive of a Wood castle.

Brackie NO 628509
This derelict L-plan tower with shotholes and bartizans bears the date 1581 and the initials of Thomas Fraser.

Brechin NO 597599
Sir Thomas Maule defended the castle for three weeks in 1303 against Edward I until killed by a missile. The present home of the Maule-Ramsey Earls of Dalhousie is of the late seventeenth and eighteenth centuries except for some cellars of a late sixteenth-century L-plan tower.

Broughty NO 465304
Lord Grey's somewhat altered tower and barmkin were licensed in 1490. The castle was partly demolished after English occupation in 1547-9 and was captured by the Catholics in 1571, and by Monck in the 1650s. It formed a coastal strongpoint in the nineteenth century and the tower is now a museum.

Careston NO 530599
Adjoining the mansion dated 1714 of Sir John Stewart of Grandtully is the Lindsays' lofty Z-planned castle with two round towers, later held by the Carnegies.

Carsegray NO 464540
The east wing of the Greys' eighteenth-century house is the Rynds' small seventeenth-century T-plan tower house.

Claypotts NO 452319 (AM)
John Strachan's Z-plan castle, with two round towers bearing square caphouses, has the dates 1569 and 1588 on it and is a particularly picturesque and unaltered specimen of its type. It was later held by the Grahams of Claverhouse.

Clova NO 322734
Little remains of the Ogilvies' tower with a round turret.

Colliston NO 612464
This Z-plan castle with two round towers, formerly with square caphouses, bears the date 1553 and the initials of John Guthrie and his second wife, M. Falconer. There is a second entrance dated 1621 and other alterations.

Cortachy NO 400594

This mansion of the Earl of Airlie contains work of many periods, the earliest parts being flanking towers remaining from Sir Walter Ogilvie's courtyard castle of about 1480.

Craig NO 704563

The Woods' square fifteenth-century inner court with two square towers has two inhabited ranges built in 1637 by the Carnegies. There is also a spacious outer court.

Dudhope NO 394307 (P, grounds only)

Two long ranges with corner towers and a twin-towered gateway remain of the courtyard mansion built about 1600 by the Scrymgeours in replacement of a tower on the same site and of the thirteenth-century Dundee Castle on lower ground to the south. It was sold to Graham of Claverhouse in 1668 and became his chief residence. He led the Jacobite rebellion of 1689 and was forfeited after his death at Killiecrankie. The castle was later a barracks and is now mostly empty.

Edzell NO 585693 (AM)

An early sixteenth-century L-plan tower stands at one corner of a ruined courtyard mansion of about 1580 with one round flanking tower. About 1600 Sir David Lindsay, Lord Edzell, added a well preserved walled garden with a summerhouse and bath-house. During the Royalist rising of 1653 John Lindsay was kidnapped from Edzell but was rescued by Cromwell's forces. It was sold to the Earl of Panmure and after his forfeiture went to the York Buildings Company. It was garrisoned in 1716 and finally abandoned in 1764.

Ethie NO 688468

The oldest parts of the existing mansion with inner and outer courts are the L-plan building in the south-west corner and the north and west ranges with a round north-west tower, these parts all being sixteenth-century and seventeenth-century work of the Carnegies, created Earls of Northesk.

Farnell NO 624555

The now restored small early sixteenth-century tower of the Bishops of Brechin was extended to the west and given a stair turret by the Carnegies or the Campbells.

Finavon NO 497566

Only the base survives of a fourteenth-century tower which was once the principal seat of the Earls of Crawford. The lofty ruined square tower is late sixteenth-century work done for Lord Lindsay of Byres. The castle returned to the Earls in 1608 and later passed to the Carnegies.

Flemington NO 527556
The derelict L-plan castle of about 1600 lies by a farmhouse.

Forter NO 183646
At the head of Glen Isla is a late sixteenth-century L-plan ruin with the wing flanking two sides of the main block. It was damaged by Argyll in 1640.

Fowlis Easter NO 321334
The Greys' lofty tower, with a round stair turret, a large chimney breast and the date 1640, is now a farmhouse. The Murrays added a north wing about 1720.

Gagie NO 448376
William Guthrie's mansion of about 1614 has two slender bartizans, and a walled garden and summerhouse to the south.

Gardyne NO 574488
The Gardynes' late sixteenth-century tower with a round stair turret was sold to James Lyell in 1682.

Glamis NO 387481 (P)
The core of the castle is a large and massive L-plan tower built for John Lyon, Lord Glamis, given the lands in 1376 along with the hand of Robert II's daughter. Patrick, Lord Glamis, created Earl of Kinghorne in 1606, remodelled the tower with an array of bartizans and dormers in place of the former battlements, and a wide new stair was provided in a round turret in the re-entrant angle. He also added the large block to the south-east with a round tower on its outer angle and in the nineteenth century this was balanced by a similar extension at the north-west corner. The Lyon Earls of Strathmore and Kinghorne still live at Glamis.

Guthrie NO 563505
This tower of the fifteenth or sixteenth century, with a stair wing and a later mansion, has always been owned by the Guthries. One of them stabbed his Gardyne cousin in a quarrel, causing a feud which brought chaos to the area for generations as each family in turn murdered the chief of the other until James VI forfeited them both. The tower then went to a junior branch of the Guthrie family.

Hatton NO 302411
Laurence, fourth Lord Oliphant, built this ruined Z-plan mansion with two square wings in 1575. It passed to the Hallyburtons in 1627 and was captured by Montrose in 1645.

Hynd NO 505416
Near Skitchen farm is a motte with traces of a tower.

Invergowrie NO 363304

The much altered house, now flats beside a hospital, is dated 1601 with the initials of Patrick Grey and Agnes Napier. It passed in 1615 to Robert Clayhills of Baldovie.

Invermark NO 443804

This remote ruined tower of the Lindsays in Glen Esk still has a yett in its entrance at hall level. The lower part is of the early sixteenth century and the upper part of about 1600.

Inverquharity NO 411579

The licence of 1444 for Alexander Ogilvy's L-plan tower specifically mentions the still surviving yett. The building was restored in the 1960s, with a gabled wing replacing the orginal demolished many years ago for its materials.

Kellie NO 608402 (P)

This lofty sixteenth-century L-plan tower was sold to the Moules in 1679 after the Royalist Irvines got into debt. It was restored and given a court to the west in the nineteenth century and is now the seat of the Earls of Dalhousie.

Kinblethmont NO 369470

In shrubs west of the mansion is the basement of an early seventeenth-century tower of the Carnegies.

Kinnaird NO 634571

The mansion of 1770 and 1854-60 contains cellars of a sixteenth-century castle of the Carnegies, created Earls of Southesk in 1633, forfeited in 1715 and restored in 1855.

Kirkbuddo NO 502435

The dormer pediment of a Guthrie castle with the initials EG is built into the farmsteading of the present house.

Lintrose NO 225379

Engulfed within the existing mansion are remains of the sixteenth-century Hallyburton castle of Fodderance.

Mains of Fintry NO 401330

This courtyard castle on the north side of Dundee was rescued from ruin in the 1970s. It has apartments on three sides and a gateway on the fourth, above which were once the date 1562 and the initials of Sir David Graham, a Catholic later executed by the Protestants. A notable feature is the lofty square stair turret bearing the date 1630 at the top.

Melgund NO 546564

Although resembling a tower house with a later, lower

145

extension, this ruin was built in one campaign about 1560 for David Bethune, a relative of Cardinal David Beaton.

Middleton NO 543487
The Gardynes' eighteenth-century mansion incorporates parts of the sixteenth-century castle.

Monikie NO 517388
On a cottage are two dormer pediments with the date 1587.

Murroes NO 461350
The Fotheringhams' sixteenth-century house with a round stair turret and gunloops is lowered and much altered.

Panmure NO 546376
Foundations of the Maules' castle lie by a ravine.

Pitairlie NO 502367
Reset on the farm offices is a stone dated 1631 with the initials of Alexander Lindsay.

Pitcur NO 252370
This ruined late sixteenth-century T-plan tower was built by the Hallyburtons.

Pitkerro NO 453337
The late sixteenth-century castle of the Durhams is long and narrow with a round stair turret and two bartizans.

Powrie NO 421346
The unusually massive Z-plan castle (one round tower is entirely destroyed) probably dates from after 1492, when a castle here was destroyed by the Scrymgeours. It was burnt by the English in 1547. The restored suite of apartments of a former courtyard is dated 1604. The lands were held by the Fotheringhams from 1412 until 1715.

Redcastle NO 688511
A thirteenth-century curtain wall isolates a small court on a headland containing a tower house of about 1500, only half of which stands above its base. The castle was captured and destroyed by the Protestants in the 1570s and was last occupied by the ousted Episcopal minister, James Rait.

Ruthven NO 302479
The sixteenth-century round tower by the walled garden is all that remains of a strongly sited Crichton castle, mostly replaced by Ogilvie of Coul's eighteenth-century mansion.

Vayne NO 493599

This ruinous Z-plan castle with one round and one square tower was built either by the Lindsays or by the Carnegies, to whom it passed in 1594. A reset tympanum has the monogram of Robert, Earl of Southesk, and others were dated 1678.

PERTH AND KINROSS DISTRICT

Aberuchill NN 744212

The L-plan castle dated 1607 of the Campbells of Lawers is now incorporated into a large mansion.

Aldie NT 050978

The Mercers' sixteenth-century tower later had its wing replaced by a longer, lower one. It was given three bartizans about 1600, and another wing was added to the first, so that the building now surrounds a tiny open court.

Ardblair NO 164446

The sixteenth-century or seventeenth-century tower of the Blairs of Balthayock has outbuildings around a small court with the arms of the Oliphants set over the gateway.

Arnot NO 207016

By the mansion is a ruined ashlar-faced fifteenth-century tower of the Arnots with one wall of the barmkin.

Ashintully NO 101613

Andro Spalding's L-plan castle has the date 1583 and the plea 'The Lord Defend This House'. It is now part of a mansion. There were several attacks on Ashintully by Highland brigands and Andro was maltreated by them in a raid in 1587.

Auchterarder NN 944134

Only some walling and some reset shotholes now remain.

Balhousie NO 116244

The dilapidated L-plan tower of the Drummonds was incorporated in the Earl of Kinnoul's mansion of 1863.

Balloch NN 784467

The nineteenth-century Taymouth Castle incorporates Sir Colin Campbell's Z-plan Balloch Castle built in the 1580s.

Balmanno NO 144156

George Auchinleck's lofty L-plan tower of about 1570-80, with a stair turret in the re-entrant angle, later passed to the Murrays and was restored by Lorimer in about 1900.

Balthayock NO 175230

Near a ravine and in the grounds of a mansion is the Blairs' derelict fifteenth-century tower. The reset date 1578 with MB and GM must refer to destroyed additions.

Balvaird NO 170115 (AM)

The fine ruined L-plan tower house with a stair turret in the re-entrant angle was probably built by Andrew Murray in the late fifteenth century. The courtyard was formerly dated 1567 on the gateway, the best preserved part of it. In 1631 Andrew Murray, minister of Abdie, succeeded to Balvaird and was created a baron in 1641 to spite the Presbyterian Kirk.

Bamff NO 222515

The Ramseys' mansion includes a sixteenth-century tower.

Belmont NO 287439

The modern mansion, now an eventide home, incorporates the Bishop of Dunkeld's small square tower of Kirkhill, later held by the Nairnes and the Mackenzies.

Blair Atholl NN 866662 (P)

The oldest part of this famous castle is the Cummings' Tower, thought to have been built by John Comyn in the 1260s. In 1457 Sir John Stewart of Balvenie was created the first of a new line of Earls of Atholl and the third Earl built the hall block adjoining the old tower. Over the centuries both portions have been greatly altered and have hardly any ancient architectural features surviving, though they contain interesting furnishings and family heirlooms. In 1745 Prince Charles Edward was at the castle, but in 1746 the Jacobite Lord George Murray besieged a government garrison in his home for seventeen days, thus making Blair Atholl the last castle in Britain to be besieged. It is still the home of the Duke of Atholl.

Braco NO 823113

This Graham mansion contains a sixteenth-century tower and work of after 1625, when one of the family was created a baronet.

Burleigh NO 140046

Adjoining an early sixteenth-century tower is one side of a court with the entrance and a round tower bearing a square caphouse dated 1582, with the initials and arms of Sir James Balfour of Mountquhanie and Margaret Balfour.

Carnbane NN 677480

On a tree-clad bluff is Red Duncan Campbell's castle of 1564.

A gateway through a ruined block led to a court behind.

Cleish NT 083978
This much altered lofty L-plan castle bears the date 1600 and the initials of Robert Colville and Beatrix Haldane, but it is clear that the strongly built lower part is earlier. A courtyard gateway is incorporated in the outbuildings.

Cluggy NN 840234
A ruined Murray castle stands on the site of a thirteenth-century Comyn promontory castle mentioned in 1467.

Clunie NO 114440
The sixteenth-century L-plan castle of the Crichtons of Elliock on an islet in the loch fell into ruin in the twentieth century.

Comrie NN 787487
The Menzies' ruined L-plan tower was built about 1580-1600.

Cowden NS 987997
All that remains is the roll-moulded courtyard gateway with bar holes and an altered little tower dated 1707.

Dowhill NT 118973
Only the cellars remain of this Lindsay castle. A tower house has been extended by an L-plan building to the west with a round tower on its outer angle. Of a court there survives just one round tower, diagonally opposite the other.

Drumlochy NO 158469
There are only traces of the Herons' castle, which was destroyed during a feud, being too close for comfort to the Blairs' castle of Glasclune on the other side of a ravine.

Drummond NN 844181 (P, gardens only)
The range containing the gateway has the dates 1630 and 1636 on it and was built for the Earl of Perth. Adjoining it is Sir John Drummond's tower of about 1490, and there is also a modern mansion. The Cromwellians damaged the castle in the 1650s and its own Jacobite owner damaged it in 1715.

Ecclesiamagirdle NO 108164
Carmichael of Balmedie's T-plan house of 1629, beside a small loch, now lies empty. A leaning courtyard gateway is dated 1648 with the initials SDC and AC.

Elcho NO 165210 (AM)
This empty castle of the Wemyss family is a fine example of a

149

defensible mansion of the mid sixteenth century, with gunports and grilles still over the windows. Two substantial square towers lie at one end, and there are round towers at a third corner and on one side opposite a crosswall. The one remaining tower of the court has the initials of Sir John Wemyss, created Earl of Wemyss in 1633.

Evelick NO 205259.
Until 1799 this ruined sixteenth-century L-plan tower with a round stair turret in the main re-entrant angle was the home of a branch of the Lindsays made baronets in 1666.

Feddal NN 824089
This ruinous Stewart mansion overlooking a ravine has old work in it and bears the date 1683.

Fingask NO 228275
The Threiplands' L-plan tower is altered and extended.

Garth NN 764504
This tower, restored in the 1960s, was where the Wolf of Badenoch died in 1394. It is strongly situated above two ravines. In the sixteenth century Nigel Stewart burnt Castle Menzies and imprisoned its laird at Garth until he signed away some of his rights. Stewart also had his own wife done to death and he ended up a prisoner for nine years within his own stronghold.

Gascon Hall NN 986175 and 995189
About a mile from the Oliphants' almost completely rebuilt castle of Old Gask are slight remains of a late tower house.

Glasclune NO 154470
The Blairs' ruined castle above a ravine is L-planned with a round tower diagonally opposite the wing.

Glendevon NN 976055
This much altered seventeenth-century Z-plan castle with two square wings and a stair turret is now a hotel. The date 1766 and the R refer to later owners, the Rutherfords.

Glendoick NO 208237
Part of Sir Thomas Murray's sixteenth-century castle now forms a rear wing of Robert Craigie's Georgian mansion.

Gleneagles NN 929093
On a knoll near the late seventeenth-century mansion are fragments of a much earlier castle of the Haldane family.

Grandtully NN 891513
The Stewarts' sixteenth-century Z-plan castle has a nearly square main block and two square wings. The date 1626 and the initials of Sir William Stewart, Sheriff of Perth, refer to additions. Because of its position the castle was used as a rendezvous by several commanders in the seventeenth and eighteenth centuries.

Ha' Tower NO 043146
Very little remains of this castle of the Grahams.

Huntingtower NO 084251 (AM)
The fifteenth-century tower of the Ruthvens was originally named after them and had a passage through its base leading to a courtyard. An L-plan tower was built close by in the sixteenth century and in the seventeenth the two were joined together. In 1582 the Earl of Gowrie and other Ruthvens abducted the young James VI from Perth to this castle in what is called the Raid of Ruthven. They then ruled in his name for several months. The King finally escaped and had the Earl beheaded in 1585. His sons were killed in their town house in Perth in 1600 during an alleged attempt on the King's life known as the Gowrie Conspiracy. Afterwards the surname Ruthven was abolished by act of Parliament and the castle renamed Huntingtower. It was later held by Murrays and the Stewarts of Atholl.

Huntly NO 301292
Andrew, Lord Grey of Foulis, was licensed to build this large and lofty L-plan tower in 1452. George Patterson added a mansion in 1800 and remodelled the old tower. It is now used as a borstal.

Inchbervie NO 123329
On a strong site are a ruined round flanking tower, a moat, a well and traces of other buildings.

Inchbrackie NN 898221
There are scanty remains of a castle destroyed in 1651.

Innerpeffrey NN 905179
This ruined L-plan castle with a square stair turret in the re-entrant angle was built about 1610 by John Drummond.

Invermay NO 061163
By the Georgian mansion is the Belshes' empty late sixteenth-century L-plan tower house.

Iverqueich NO 277497
On a strong site is a ruined enclosure where Edward I stayed

in 1296. It was granted in 1394 to James Lindsay.

Keltie NO 008133
The L-plan castle of the Bonars, and later the Drummonds and the Airlies, has a bartizan set halfway up a corner.

Kenmore NN 766454
An island priory in the loch, fortified by the Campbells, was besieged in turn by Montrose and General Monck.

Kincardine NO 946110
Near the modern mansion are scanty remains of a courtyard castle of the Grahams dismantled by Argyll in 1645.

Kinclaven NO 158377
Hidden in trees by the junction of the Tay and the Isla are ruins of a square castle of enclosure formerly with corner towers, probably built by Alexander II. It was held by the English in 1297 and 1335 and was dismantled afterwards.

Kinnaird NO 242291
The Kinnairds' lofty restored fifteenth-century tower has a buttress carried up as a turret. The nearby kitchen has the date 1610 and the initials of Sir Patrick Threipland. The two lie on a promontory above a stream.

Lethendy NO 140417
Beside the Victorian mansion is the Herons' L-plan tower, which is earlier than the year 1678, which it bears.

Lochearnhead NN 690243
On the tree-clad Neishes' Island are relics of a castle.

Loch Leven NO 138018
This was a thirteenth-century courtyard castle occupying the whole of an islet in Loch Leven until the water level was lowered. Alan de Vipont held it against the English forces aiding Edward Balliol in 1335. A tower house was added in the late fourteenth century and the outer wall was rebuilt, given a round tower and various internal buildings in the sixteenth century. In 1567 Queen Mary was kept here for nearly a year, during which she signed her abdication and gave birth to stillborn twins by Bothwell.

Meggernie NN 554460
Colin Campbell's tower house of 1580, in which he held the abducted Countess of Erroll, has square bartizans and now adjoins a later mansion. It was held later by the Menzies.

Megginch NO 242246
Sir George Hay sold this castle in the seventeenth century to John Drummond of Lennoch, whose descendants are still there. The core of the house is a sixteenth-century tower having a round stair turret with a square caphouse amid one side.

Menzies NN 837496 (P)
The castle is a large Z-plan building with two square wings and is dated 1577 with the initials of James Menzies and Barbara Stewart, a marriage indicating that rival families were now reconciled. There is probably an older tower incorporated; there are additions of 1840, and the Clan Menzies is in the 1980s completing restoration work.

Methven NO 042261
Ludovick, Duke of Lennox's mid seventeenth-century mansion with bartizans incorporates earlier work.

Moncur NO 284295
Hidden by trees from the nearby road is a ruined sixteenth-century Z-plan castle with one round and one square tower.

Monzie NN 873245
The mansion has at the rear an L-plan castle dated 1634, though possibly built slightly earlier.

Moredun Hall NO 145193
There are slight traces of the Moncrieffes' castle.

Moulin (or Black Castle) NN 946589
Only fragments remain of a small courtyard castle with round corner towers, built in 1326 by Sir John Campbell on what was then an island in a loch. It was used only until 1512.

Murthly NO 070399
A small tower was later given bartizans and in about 1620 a wing by the Stewarts of Grandtully. It now lies at one corner of a large mansion.

Newton NO 172453
This Drummond Z-plan castle of the late sixteenth century has one round tower and one square one.

Ogilvie NO 909081
Above a ravine are remains of a Graham castle.

Pitfour NO 200209
The mansion of 1829 incorporates a medieval nucleus and

work done for the Hays in 1784. There is also a dovecot.

Pitheavlis NO 097222
The sixteenth-century L-plan tower is still inhabited.

Rohallion NO 039401
The remains of a tiny Z-plan castle with two round turrets lie hidden among bracken high up on a hillside.

Stobhall NO 132344
After 1487 Stobhall was a dower house of the Drummonds of Drummond Castle. Above the Tay are a group of modest sixteenth-century buildings set irregularly around a courtyard.

Strathallan NN 919156
The house includes parts of a Drummond castle.

Struie NO 179114
In a garden is a round stair turret with shotholes.

The Ward NO 109442
West of Clunie Loch are fragments of an early enclosure.

Trochrie NO 978402
Only part of the stair turret of this castle of the Ruthvens of Gowrie survives in a garden behind a house.

Tullibole NO 053006
This fine house with a stair wing on one side bears the date 1608 and initials of John Haliday and Helen Oliphant.

Whitefield NO 089617
This ruined Spalding castle was similar to neighbouring Ashintully with a wing flanking two sides of the main block. It remained intact until the early nineteenth century.

Williamstoun NO 972220
This late tower with a stair turret surmounted by a caphouse was built for Oliphant of Gask's disinherited heir.

The Western Isles

Bheagram NF 761371
An islet in Loch an Eilean bears a small ruined tower.

Borve NF 774506
Three walls remain of a large early Macdonald tower house.

Calvey NF 817182

On an islet off Calvey Island is a ruined undated court with one tiny square tower and two ranges of apartments.

Kiesimul NL 665979

On an islet in Castle Bay is the castle of the Macneils of Barra, restored in the 1950s by their American descendant. The date of its construction is hotly debated, the high but thin courtyard wall being probably of the late thirteenth century and an addition to a slightly earlier tower keep. The internal buildings are sixteenth-century work and later.

Sinclair NL 648996

A tiny tower lies on an islet in Loch Tangusdale on Barra.

Glossary of architectural terms

Ashlar: masonry of blocks wrought to even faces and square edges.

Bailey: a court surrounded by a defensive perimeter.

Barmkin: a small enclosure of modest defensive strength.

Bartizan: a turret corbelled out from near the top of a wall or tower, usually at a corner.

Bastion: a projection from a wall to give flanking fire. Of a lower profile and often larger than a tower.

Bottle dungeon: a deep prison accessible only from above.

Caphouse: a small chamber at the head of a wing or stair.

Caponier: a vaulted chamber providing the bottom of a ditch with flanking fire.

Chamfer: a surface formed by cutting off a square edge, usually at an angle of forty-five degrees.

Chemise: an enclosure with its wall fairly closely surrounding a central block.

Citadel: the ultimate strongpoint.

Corbel: a projection of stone jutting out from a wall to support a timber beam or other stonework, as in a parapet or bartizan.

Curtain wall: the high enclosing wall around a bailey.

Dormer window: a window standing up vertically from the slope of a roof, usually in the same plane as the outer face of the walling below.

Fortalice: an old Scots term for a stronghold of medium size and defensive strength.

Hall house: a house usually of two storeys with the principal apartments end-to-end on one level instead of one above the other as in a tower house.

Harling: plaster mixed with coarse aggregate such as gravel and applied to the outside walls as a weather protection. The same as rough-cast.

Keep-gatehouse: a gateway with the additional functions of principal residence and ultimate stronghold.

Machicolation: an opening either below a projecting parapet or bartizan or in the vault of an entrance passage to allow missiles to be dropped or fired on assailants.

Motte: a castle mound, usually at least partly artificial.

Moulding: ornament of continuous section.

Oriel: a bay window projected out above ground level on corbels, mouldings or a plain masonry projection.

Palace house: similar to a hall house, though with less emphasis on defence than in the earlier hall houses.

Parapet: a wall for protection at any sudden drop, as on a bridge or on the summit of castle walls and towers.

Pediment: a formalised gable used over doorways and windows, especially dormer windows.

Pele: a timber fort.

Pele house: a modestly sized semi-defensible house of two storeys with a gabled roof. Also called a bastle house or stronghouse. Derived from pele tower, a modest tower house with a timber barmkin in the border area.

Portcullis: a gate usually made of wood reinforced with iron designed to rise and fall in vertical grooves at the entry to a castle. Not used in Scottish tower houses but found in early courtyard castles.

Postern: a lesser gateway or back entrance.

Quoins: dressed stones at the corners of a building.

Rib vault: a vault supported by, or decorated with, ribs.

Skewstone or skewputt: the bottom bracket of a characteristically Scottish stepped gable.

Wall-walk: a walkway on top of a castle wall or tower.

Yett: a strong hinged gate made of interwoven iron bars.

Further reading

Cruden, Stewart. *The Scottish Castle*. Nelson, 1960.

Fry, P. S. *Castles*. David and Charles, 1980.

Graham, Cuthbert. *Grampian — The Castle Country*. Grampian Regional Council, 1982.

McGibbon, David, and Ross, Thomas. *The Castellated and Domestic Architecture of Scotland*. Five volumes. David Douglas, 1883-92; reprint by James Thin, 1977.

Tranter, Nigel. *The Heartland. The Eastern Counties. The North East*. Three volumes of the Queen's Scotland series. Hodder and Stoughton, 1971, 1972, 1974.

Tranter, Nigel. *The Fortified House in Scotland*. Four volumes. Oliver and Boyd, 1962-6.

See also the relevant volumes of the Royal Commission on Historical Monuments and the Annual Proceedings of the Society of Antiquaries of Scotland.

Index

158

INDEX